Day Hike!

COLUMBIA GORGE

Day Hike!

COLUMBIA GORGE

2nd Edition

Seabury Blair Jr.

SASQUATCH BOOKS
SEATTLE

Printed in the United States of America
Published by Sasquatch Books
Distributed by PGW/Perseus
17 16 15 14 13 12 11   9 8 7 6 5 4 3 2 1

Cover photograph: Ed Books/edbookphoto.com
Cover design: Sarah Plein and Rosebud Eustace
Interior design: Jenny Wilkson
Interior composition: Rachelle Longé and Liza Brice-Dahmen
Interior photographs: Seabury Blair Jr.
Interior maps: Marlene Blair

Library of Congress Cataloging-in-Publication Data is available.

ISBN-13: 978-1-57061-729-4
ISBN-10: 1-57061-729-5

Important Note: Please use common sense. No guidebook can act as a substitute for
experience, careful planning, the right equipment, and appropriate training. There is inherent
danger in all activities described in this book, and readers must assume full responsibility for
their own actions and safety. Changing or unfavorable conditions in weather, roads, trails,
snow, waterways, and so forth cannot be anticipated by the author or publisher, but should
be considered by any outdoor participants. The author and publisher will not be responsible
for the safety of the users of this guide.

Sasquatch Books
119 South Main Street, Suite 400
Seattle, WA 98104
(206) 467-4300
www.sasquatchbooks.com
custserv@sasquatchbooks.com

CONTENTS

CONTENTS

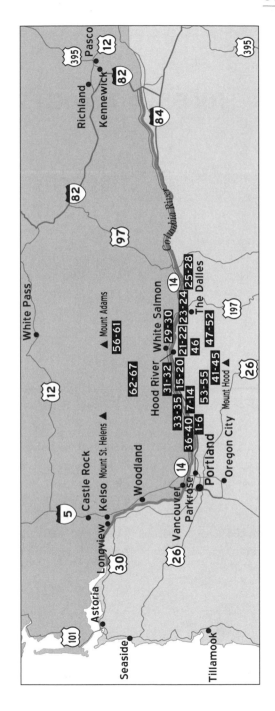

HIKES AT A GLANCE

Easy

NO.	HIKE NAME	RATING	BEST SEASON	KIDS	DOGS
1	Rooster Rock Loop	🚶	Fall, winter	✓	✓
10	Gorge Trail No. 400, Eagle Creek–Bridge of the Gods	🚶🚶	Winter	✓	✓
11	Gorge Trail No. 400, Tanner Creek–McCord Creek	🚶🚶	Winter	✓	✓
18	Mount Defiance (Easy Way)	🚶🚶🚶🚶	Summer	✓	✓
20	Columbia River Highway–Viento State Park	🚶🚶	Winter	✓	✓
24	Rowena Plateau	🚶🚶🚶	Spring	✓	
34	The Dam Loop	🚶	Spring	✓	✓
36	Sams-Walker Picnic Area	🚶	Spring	✓	✓
37	St. Cloud Picnic Loops	🚶	Spring	✓	✓
51	Lookout Mountain (Easy Way)	🚶🚶🚶🚶🚶	Summer		✓
53	Lost Lake Loop	🚶🚶🚶	Late fall, summer	✓	✓
62	Mineral Springs Loop	🚶🚶	Fall, summer	✓	✓

Moderate

NO.	HIKE NAME	RATING	BEST SEASON	KIDS	DOGS
2	Latourell Falls Loop	🚶🚶🚶	Spring	✓	✓
8	Gorge Trail No. 400, Eagle Creek–Tanner Creek	🚶🚶	Fall	✓	✓
12	Wahclella Falls Loop	🚶🚶🚶	Spring	✓	✓
13	Eagle Creek Trail No. 440	🚶🚶🚶🚶	Fall, spring		✓
14	Pacific Crest Trail 2000, Cascade Locks–Dry Creek Falls	🚶🚶🚶	Spring, fall	✓	✓
15	Herman Creek Pinnacles	🚶🚶	Fall, winter	✓	✓
16	Herman Creek Trail	🚶🚶🚶🚶	Summer		✓
22	Wygant Viewpoint	🚶🚶🚶	Spring, fall	✓	✓
25	Columbia River Highway Trail	🚶🚶🚶🚶	Spring, fall	✓	✓
26	Dalles Riverfront Trail	🚶🚶🚶🚶	Spring, fall	✓	✓
28	Deschutes River Rail Trail	🚶🚶🚶🚶	Spring, fall	✓	✓
29	Klickitat Rail Trail	🚶🚶🚶🚶	Spring, fall	✓	✓
30	Catherine Creek	🚶🚶🚶🚶	Spring		✓

NO.	HIKE NAME	RATING	BEST SEASON	KIDS	DOGS
33	Pacific Crest Trail 2000, Gillette Lake	🚶🚶	Spring, fall	✔	✔
38	Hardy and Rodney Falls	🚶🚶🚶	Spring, fall	✔	✔
40	Beacon Rock	🚶🚶🚶🚶	Summer, spring	✔	✔
47	Tamanawas Falls from Sherwood	🚶🚶🚶	Fall, summer	✔	✔
48	Tamanawas Falls Loop	🚶🚶🚶	Fall, summer		✔
49	Horsethief Meadows	🚶🚶🚶	Fall, summer	✔	✔
52	Palisade Point	🚶🚶🚶🚶	Summer		✔
56	Bird Creek Meadows	🚶🚶🚶	Summer, fall	✔	✔
59	Salt Creek Trail	🚶🚶	Summer, fall	✔	✔
65	Blue Lake	🚶🚶🚶🚶	Summer	✔	✔
67	Falls Creek Falls	🚶🚶🚶	Summer, fall	✔	✔

Moderately Difficult

NO.	HIKE NAME	RATING	BEST SEASON	KIDS	DOGS
3	Angel's Rest	🚶🚶🚶🚶	Fall, early summer		✔
4	Wahkeena Falls Loop	🚶🚶🚶🚶🚶	Spring, fall		✔
5	Gorge Trail No. 400, Triple Falls	🚶🚶🚶🚶	Spring, fall	✔	✔
6	Larch Mountain Loop	🚶🚶🚶🚶	Fall	✔	✔
7	Wauna Viewpoint	🚶🚶🚶	Fall	✔	✔
19	Starvation Creek Loop	🚶🚶🚶	Fall		✔
23	McCall Point	🚶🚶🚶🚶	Spring	✔	
27	Deschutes River Loop	🚶🚶🚶🚶	Spring, fall	✔	✔
35	Wind Mountain	🚶🚶🚶	Spring, summer	✔	✔
41	Tilly Jane Loop	🚶🚶🚶🚶	Fall, summer	✔	✔
43	Lamberson Butte	🚶🚶🚶🚶	Fall, summer		✔
44	Timberline Trail No. 600, West	🚶🚶🚶	Fall, summer	✔	✔
45	Polallie Ridge Loop	🚶🚶🚶	Fall, summer	✔	✔
46	Bald Butte	🚶🚶🚶	Spring, fall		✔
50	Lookout Mountain (Hard Way)	🚶🚶🚶🚶🚶	Summer		✔
54	Lost Lake Butte	🚶🚶🚶🚶	Fall, summer		✔
55	Huckleberry Mountain Trail	🚶🚶🚶	Summer, fall		✔
58	Crofton Ridge	🚶🚶🚶	Summer, fall		✔
66	Race Track via Pacific Crest Trail 2000	🚶🚶🚶🚶	Fall, summer	✔	✔

Difficult

NO.	HIKE NAME	RATING	BEST SEASON	KIDS	DOGS
9	Ruckel Creek Trail No. 405	🚶🚶🚶	Summer		✔
21	Mitchell Point	🚶🚶🚶	Spring		✔

HIKES AT A GLANCE

No.	Hike	Rating	Best Season	Dogs
31	Dog Mountain Trail No. 147	🚶🚶🚶🚶	Spring, fall	✔
32	Dog Mountain Trail No. 4407	🚶🚶🚶	Spring, fall	✔
39	Hamilton Mountain	🚶🚶🚶🚶🚶	Summer, fall	✔
42	Cooper Spur	🚶🚶🚶🚶🚶	Fall, summer	✔
57	Crescent Glacier	🚶🚶🚶🚶	Summer, fall	✔
60	Horseshoe Meadow	🚶🚶🚶	Summer, fall	✔
61	Snipes Mountain Trail No. 11	🚶🚶🚶	Summer, fall	✔
63	Soda Peaks Lake Trail No. 133	🚶🚶🚶	Summer, fall	✔
64	Little Huckleberry Mountain	🚶🚶🚶🚶	Summer, fall	✔

Extreme

NO.	HIKE NAME	RATING	BEST SEASON	KIDS	DOGS
17	Mount Defiance (Hard Way)	🚶🚶🚶	Summer		✔

ACKNOWLEDGMENTS

As always, I am most grateful to all of the U.S. Forest Service trail crews and volunteers who make day-hiking a pleasant experience for all of us—and a great job for me. Thanks, too, to my wife, Marlene (aka B. B. Hardbody), for her love, support, and the excellent maps included in this book. And, of course, thanks to Gary Luke and the sharp-eyed editors at Sasquatch Books.

INTRODUCTION

My first memories of the Columbia Gorge date from a family outing to Seaside, Oregon, in 1949. Dad and Mom piled my brother
and me into the 1946 Plymouth and headed across Horse Heaven
Hills from Spokane to motor along the beautiful Columbia River
Highway. We stopped at Multnomah Falls—who doesn't?—and
climbed up the trail to gawk. I don't remember much about that
splendid cascade but can recount to this day exactly how many
streamlined Pullmans passed by below, tugged along by an early
Union Pacific diesel-electric engine.

It wasn't until the spring of 1961 that I returned to the Gorge to
spend a couple of nights with Ted Sperry's family in their White
Salmon home overlooking the shining Columbia. Though I dimly
recall a spectacular sunset glowing off Mount Hood, the clearest
memory I have of that trip was of my college friend's wooden skis
slipping out of the rack and catching fire on the Beetle's exhaust
pipe as we drove to Bend. That and the encounter we had with a
snowdrift at Timberline Lodge, when Sperry sliced his finger trying
to dig snow from the broken headlight and piloted the VW all the
way to Deschutes Crossing with the only bandage we had—a piece
of Wonderbread—wrapped around his digit.

So I didn't discover the day-hiking treasure of the Columbia
Gorge until nearly five decades later, when I coaxed my old body
and constant companion, Stummick, into walking all of the trails
in this book. Incidentally, though Stummick growled on every
hike, he always arrived at trail's end in front of me. I commuted
from my West Puget Sound home to the Gorge, camping at Trout
Lake and Ainsworth, Memaloose and Deschutes River state parks.
I hiked three and sometimes four days a week, often tromping two
trails a day. Except for a couple of hot, dry days on Mount Adams,
it was a great way to spend the summer and fall.

Indeed, the Gorge, the south side of Mount Adams, and the north
side of Mount Hood serve up some of the best day-hiking in the
nation. Most trails are well-maintained and share a trait that we
who take our woodland walks in daily chunks appreciate: You get
all of your uphill sweating out of the way the first half of the hike.

Another plus for wildland pedestrians: Most of you are no more than ninety minutes from the farthest-flung trailhead. That means more time to photograph wildflowers, admire the view, explore the waterfalls, and slap at mosquitoes. Now, get out there and start making your own memories, sure to be more vivid than mine.

–Seabury Blair Jr.

USING THIS GUIDE

The beginning of each trail description is intended to give you quick information that can help you decide whether the specific day hike is one that interests you. Here's what you'll find:

Trail Number & Name

Trails are numbered in this guide following a geographical order; see the Overview Map on page vii for general location. Trail names usually reflect those names used by the national forest service and other land managers. In some cases, portions of very long trails or multiple sections of separate trails have been combined into a single hike and assigned a new name.

Overall Rating

Assigning an overall rating to a hike is a difficult task given the fact that one hiker's preferred trail is another's dungheap. Yet every hike in this guide is worth taking (we're still working on the dungheap trail guide). Here, the difference between a five-star hike and one with four stars might only be the number and variety of wildflowers along the trail, or the height of the tripping tree roots arrayed on the path before you. The trails in this book are the best you'll find in the Columbia Gorge, the north side of Mount Hood, and the south side of Mount Adams. Some might not be as good as others, but they are all better than the trails we've excluded.

Another problem is attempting to be objective in rating the trails. Some of us are pushovers for trails above timberline, where the wildflowers wave in gentle summer breezes, where mountains claw clouds, and where cooling snowfields linger through summer. Hikes with these features may be rated higher than you might rate them. If you're a hiker who loves walking along rattling rivers, or padding on leafy trails softened by mosses while trying to find the sky through a canopy of 300-foot-tall evergreens, you might add one star to every forest hike listed here, and subtract one star from every alpine hike.

Finally, many factors must be considered in assigning an overall rating. Besides all that aesthetic stuff like scenery and wildlife, there are objective criteria like trail condition, length, and steepness, and obstacles like creek crossings or deadfall. On the other hand, you can forget all that junk and just take our word for it:

🏃 This hike is worth taking, even with your in-laws.

🏃🏃 Expect to discover socially and culturally redeeming values on this hike. Or, at least, very fine scenery.

🏃🏃🏃 You would be willing to get up before sunrise to take this hike, even if you watched all of Letterman the night before.

🏃🏃🏃🏃 Here is the Häagen-Dazs of hikes; if you don't like ice cream, a hike with this rating will give more pleasure than any favorite comfort food.

🏃🏃🏃🏃🏃 The aesthetic and physical rewards are so great that hikes given this rating are forbidden by most conservative religions.

Distance

The distance listed is round-trip, exclusive of any side trips to awesome waterfalls or other features mentioned along the way. If these excursions off the main trail are longer than about 0.2 mile, that distance will be mentioned in the description of the hike.

Hiking Time

This is an estimate of the time it takes the average hiker to walk the trail, round-trip. Because none of us are average hikers, you may feel free to ignore this entry. For the most part, however, the pace on the trail is calculated at 2 miles per hour. Times are estimated conservatively; even so, this rate might slow on trails with significant elevation gain. (Some hikers will wonder what sort of trail slug came up with such ridiculously long hiking times—and we're okay with that.)

Elevation Gain

This is a calculation of the total number of feet you'll have to climb on the trail. Don't assume that all of the elevation will be gained on the way to your destination—although this is often the case with Columbia Gorge trails. Some of these trails actually lose elevation on the way and gain it on the return, or alternately gain and lose elevation along the way. The certainty is that on a round-trip hike, you always gain the same amount of elevation that you lose.

High Point

This is the highest point above sea level you'll reach on any given hike.

Difficulty Level

Here's another tough one. Experienced hikers might find a walk rated "Moderately Difficult" to be only "Moderate," while beginning trekkers might rate the same hike "Difficult." As with the hiking times, noted earlier, the difficulty of individual hikes was rated conservatively.

The terms used here are:

EASY: Few, if any, hills; generally between 1 and 3 miles, round-trip; suitable for families with small children.

MODERATE: Longer, gently graded hills; generally between 3 and 5 miles long, round-trip.

MODERATELY DIFFICULT: Steeper grades; elevation changes greater than about 1,000 feet; between 5 and 8 miles long, round-trip.

DIFFICULT: Sustained, steep climbs of at least 1 mile; elevation gain and loss greater than 1,500 feet; usually more than 8 miles long, round-trip. Your deodorant may fail you on these hikes.

EXTREME: Sustained, steep climbs; distances greater than 9 miles, round-trip. These trails will rigorously test your hiking skills and muscles.

Best Season

Here you'll find our recommendation for the best time of year to take any given hike, ranked by preferred season. Trails that are open throughout the year or that make good three-season hikes will be noted here.

Permits/Contact

This entry will tell you whether you need a Northwest Forest Pass or other permit and which land manager to contact for more information.

Maps

The two most popular types of maps, United States Geological Survey (USGS) "quads" and Green Trails, are listed for each hike when both are available. Maps are available at outdoor retailers such as REI, at some bookstores in the Gorge, and at most Forest Service visitor centers. Many hikers now use Internet map servers (such as http://mapserver.maptech.com) to download USGS maps, or print their own customized maps from CD-ROM software.

Each hike in this book includes a trail map of the route, featuring parking and trailhead, alternate routes, direction, elevation profile, and more. Our maps are based most often on USGS; use the following legend:

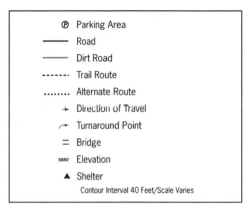

℗	Parking Area
——	Road
——	Dirt Road
------	Trail Route
....	Alternate Route
⇀	Direction of Travel
⌒	Turnaround Point
=	Bridge
5880'	Elevation
▲	Shelter
	Contour Interval 40 Feet/Scale Varies

Trail Notes

Look here for a quick guide to trail regulations and features: leashed dogs okay; dogs prohibited; kid-friendly; and bikes allowed.

After the at-a-glance overview of each hike, you'll find detailed descriptions of the following:

The Hike

This section is an attempt to convey the feel of the trail in a sentence or two, including the type of trail and whether there's a one-way hiking option.

Getting There

You'll either find out how to get to the trailhead or, God forbid, become hopelessly lost. The elevation at the trailhead is also included here.

The main access highway for all these hikes is Interstate 84 in Oregon, although the trails can also be reached via Highway 14 in Washington. We've included directions for each when it might be a driver's preference. The main access highway for the section on the north side of Mount Hood is Highway 35; for the south side of Mount Adams, it is Highway 141 and the Wind River Road.

The hikes outlined in this book are also possible in a long day or weekend outing for wildland pedestrians from the Greater Puget Sound area. Although Interstate 5 is the likely route, I found Forest Road 23 from Randle to Trout Lake to be a much more pleasant alternative—and nearly as fast to trails at Mount Adams and the eastern end of the Gorge. The road is paved for all but 17 miles—and only about two of those are really bad—from Randle to Trout Lake. Seattle and Tacoma hikers may want to take the Skate Creek Road south from Ashford to Packwood, then follow Highway 12 west to Randle and FR 23.

The Trail

Here's where you'll get the blow-by-blow, mile-by-mile description of the trail. It's information your feet will find useful, and we apologize if, every now and then, we take time to recognize an awesome waterfall or a good view, since you'll probably recognize these features without much coaching.

Going Farther

In this section, you can learn about good options to take a longer hike along the same trail. Interesting side trips can be found here, too. And if there's a nearby campground that could get you on the trail sooner, or a great place to stay while exploring area trails, it also will be mentioned. Not every hike includes this section.

BE CAREFUL

It is all too easy on a warm, sunny day on the trail to forget all of the stuff you ought to be carrying in your pack. Day hikers, especially, are likely to leave that extra layer or waterproof breathable parka in the trunk. Some folks even forget that most essential item—a hiking partner. We all know we shouldn't hike alone.

In almost all cases, day hikers who forget one or two of the basic rules for safe wilderness travel return to the trailhead smiling and healthy. No trail cop is going to cite you for negligent hiking if you have only nine of the so-called "Ten Essential Systems," or if you hit the trail without registering or telling someone where you're going.

Perhaps the only weighty argument anyone can make to convince another day hiker to follow the rules for safe travel in the outdoors is this: Remember the annual, avoidable tragedies that occur because hikers ignore those rules—and become news headlines instead.

The Ten Essential Systems

Those clever Mountaineers are always certain to stay abreast of the latest trend. Today we live in a world of "systems"—as in "life support systems" or "total system failure"—so the Seattle-based Mountaineers organization, which came up with the original Ten Essentials, has modified the list to the Ten Essential Systems. This fact was called to my attention by a member of the Mountaineers who serves on the club's Subcommittee of the Committee to Change the Names of Everything Familiar So As to Befuddle and Confuse Old Hikers. These new essential systems include:

1. A navigation system, which might include a global positioning system (GPS) instead of a map and compass. If you choose a GPS, make certain to carry a spare energy system (battery) along. I'd advise carrying a topographic map system as well. A GPS can tell you where you are and where to go, but it can't tell you that your next step will be off a cliff. I suppose under most circumstances you'd know that.

2. A sun protection system, which might include sunglasses, sunscreen, and one of those big picnic-table umbrellas.

3. An insulation system, defined in the old Ten Essentials as "extra clothing." It might be a top and bottom insulating layer and a waterproof and windproof top layer, as well as a hat or cap. Or you might prefer an insulation system that includes a body-sized box made from rigid foam insulation. It would be light enough to tote on day hikes and would also serve as an emergency shelter system.

4. An illumination system, once known as a flashlight with an extra bulb and batteries. Alternative illumination systems might include a carbide miner's lamp or emergency flares—which could double as your fire system. Headlamps with light-emitting diodes (LEDs) and lithium batteries burn longer than other systems but may also deplete your financial accounting system.

5. A first-aid system was formerly defined as a first-aid kit, but you might prefer to drag your personal physician along. I suppose a nurse would do just as well, except in emergencies that might involve surgical procedures. If your first aid system doesn't include wraps for sprains, add an ankle support system and be sure you have some kind of blister treatment system.

6. A fire system, once described as waterproof matches and a firestarter. If your illumination system consists of a couple of emergency flares, you can probably skip this one.

7. A repair and tools system. The Ten Essentials said a pocket knife would do, but with today's technology no single Swiss Army knife can open every type of beer container.

8. A nutrition system, once defined as extra food.

9. A hydration system, known as "water" in the obsolete parlance.

10. An emergency shelter system, which should be no problem if you opt for a rigid foam insulation system. One of those lightweight plastic/foil blankets or bags might work better.

In addition to these items, most day hikers never hit the trail without toting a toilet paper system in a plastic bag and perhaps some type of bug repellent on summer hikes. A loud emergency whistle is a lightweight addition. Binoculars are worth their weight simply for watching wildlife, and might help you find your route if you become lost. Consider, too, a walking stick or a trekking pole of some variety; it can take the stress off your knees on steep downhills, help steady you while crossing streams, and serve a wide variety of other useful purposes, such as a support post for a portable lean-to should you need emergency shelter.

Water

Dehydration is one of the most common ailments that day hikers face. No one should head out on the trail without at least one liter of clean water per person.

You'll find plenty of opportunities to refill your water bottle on most of the hikes outlined in this book. In cases where creek crossings are scarce or obtaining water might be a problem, it will be mentioned in the trail description.

Treat all water in the outdoors as if it were contaminated. The most worrisome problem might be a little critter called *Giardia lamblia*, which can give you a case of the trots that you'll never forget. The most noticeable symptom of giardiasis is "explosive diarrhea." Need you know more? Probably not.

Thankfully, there is an easy way to assure that the water you take from Northwest streams and lakes is safe to drink. When used properly, filter pumps eliminate at least 99.9 percent of giardia and other dangerous organisms from the water. A recent and far more convenient addition to filter pumps, especially for day hikers, are the relatively inexpensive water bottles equipped with their own filters. You simply fill the bottle from the stream (taking extreme care not to contaminate the mouthpiece or drinking cap), drop the filter into place, screw on the top, and you're ready to drink filtered water. Conversely, many veteran hikers choose to forego all this gadgetry and use the old-fashioned method: iodine water treatments, which come in tablets or crystals. The taste might be objectionable to some, but it's a guaranteed way to kill giardia and other waterborne bugs—something a filter, especially an improperly used or maintained one, is not. Of course, the downside to iodine treatment is the wait for the tablet to dissolve in cold mountain water, often as long as twenty minutes.

Weather

In any area weather can change rapidly and with little warning. In the Columbia Gorge wind is the most likely weather phenomenon you'll encounter—almost daily. Always carry a windproof layer of clothing and look for winds from the east or west to increase in the afternoon. On most any alpine hike on Mount Adams or Mount Hood, you can get snowed on, rained on, sleeted on, blown around, and finally sunburned—all in the span of a single day. Hikers on Hood and Adams have frozen to death in freak summer storms and slipped off cliffs in Gorge rainstorms. Mother Nature is most often a friendly, generous old lady who bakes cookies and bread for you, but when you least expect it, she puts on a goalie's mask and whacks at you with an icicle or lightning bolt.

So be prepared, scouts.

Rain is another likely weather-related hazard. In the alpine country of Mount Adams and Mount Hood, rain combined with wind adds up to hypothermia. Waterproof, windproof gear can save your life. On rainy lowland trails, the only sure way to stay dry in a serious rainfall is to stay at home. If you hike on these days, simply consider dampness to be a hiking partner and stow some dry clothes in the car.

Flora & Fauna

Two of the most significant dangers in the Columbia Gorge are poison oak and rattlesnakes. Both are most likely found in the eastern sections of the Gorge, and both are easily avoided.

Poison oak is readily identified by its shiny green leaves, which grow in threes. It grows mostly on sunny, exposed slopes in great clumps covering wide areas and sometimes lines hiking trails like the Dog Mountain pathways (see hikes #31 and #32). It is most virulent in the late spring and summer and can cause a rash of blisters on hikers most sensitive to the toxic oil. Worse, the poison can get onto your clothing and even spread to other clothing in the wash. Fido can pick the poison up on his coat and, as with fleas, bring it home to you.

But today, modern science has come to our rescue with a product called Tecnu. It's a lotion that neutralizes the toxic oil of poison oak, both before and after you've been exposed. The easiest way to use it, I learned from experienced itchers and scratchers, is to slather it on after you return from your hike, let it work a minute, then wipe it off. Mount Hood forest rangers also told me they apply Tecnu before they leave the office and it protects them in the woods all day. One said an alternative to Tecnu is the goo mechanics use to clean grease from their hands—but I was too chicken to test his assertion. You can buy Tecnu at most drugstores and outdoor-gear retailers in the Columbia Gorge.

Rattlesnakes frequently hold conventions on the sunny slopes of Dog Mountain or along the Deschutes River trails (see hikes #27 and #28) and are most active during the hot summer months. Despite large numbers of these poisonous reptiles, very few hikers are ever bitten; death from a rattlesnake bite is extremely rare.

Snakes, including rattlers, are not aggressive and will always slither off if given the opportunity. The best advice: Don't put your hands or feet anywhere you can't see them, except into your pockets or boots.

Although black bears and cougars roam the woods of the Columbia Gorge and surrounding mountains, encounters aren't likely. Black bears are mostly a nuisance, and while cougars may occasionally treat humans as prey, you'll probably never see one on the trail. If you do see a bear or a cougar, heed the following advice from the Washington Department of Fish and Wildlife:

Bear: Give the bear plenty of room to get away. Never get between a cub and its mother. Avoid eye contact but speak softly to the bear while backing away from it. Try not to show fear and don't turn your back on a bear. If you can't get away from it, clap your hands or yell in an effort to scare it away. If the bear becomes aggressive, fight back using anything at your disposal. Should the attack continue, curl up in a ball or lay down on your stomach and play dead.

Cougar: Don't take your eyes off the cougar. Make yourself appear big by raising your arms above your head, open your jacket if you're wearing one, and wave a stick above your head. If the cougar approaches, yell and throw rocks, sticks, anything you can get your hands on. In the event of an attack, fight back aggressively.

Less dangerous but more common hazards to day hikers include stinging and biting pests like yellow jackets, particularly in late summer and early fall, and black flies, mosquitoes, and deer flies. Liberal doses of insect repellent (those with at least some percentage of the chemical DEET are most effective) can take care of the mosquitoes and deer flies but probably won't keep those pesky yellow jackets away.

Of course, none of these warnings should be construed as discouragement. We've been hiking around the Northwest for a lifetime and have yet to get lost in a snowstorm or be menaced by wild animals, attacked by killer bees, or swept away in a glacial runoff. So tighten your bootlaces, shoulder that pack, and get out on one of the hikes that follow. Shoot, get out on a bunch of them.

Etiquette/Ethics

To protect this wonderful landscape so that users in future generations can enjoy it just as much as you, please follow a few simple rules. Stay on established trails, don't cut switchbacks, and stay off sensitive areas. Leave no trace, pack out your trash, and respect other trail users. And because you're having such a great time using the trails of the Northwest, why not volunteer your services by lending a hand on a trail-building or repair project?

Happy trails!

THE COLUMBIA GORGE

The Columbia Gorge from Portland, Oregon, to the mouth of the
Deschutes River offers varied terrain for day hikers.

THE COLUMBIA GORGE

Welcome to Lewis and Clark country and the river that led the explorers to the end of their journey. Although Meriwether Lewis and William Clark likely had enough of walking by the time they reached Rockfort, near The Dalles, in October 1805, your journey is just beginning. The Corps of Discovery probably had no notion that in about two hundred years, this green and golden land would give us some of America's best trails to hike in a day—no inkling that we now consider recreation something over which they toiled and sweated for three years.

Perhaps nowhere in the nation can you find an area that offers such diversity to the day hiker. In fewer than two hours, you can drive from sea to glacier level, stroll through a rain forest, walk through a desert, or admire awesome waterfalls, among the highest in North America. You can hike along riverside plateaus purple with grass widows in the spring and wander orange and golden oak forests in the fall. You can slip and slide on summer snow on the mountains Native American tribes called Klickitat and Wy'east— Mount Adams and Mount Hood.

For day hikers, the Gorge might be considered the area that stretches upriver from the suburbs of Portland, Oregon, and Vancouver, Washington, to the mouth of the Deschutes River in Oregon and the Klickitat River in Washington. That's fewer than 80 miles, but you can expect dramatic changes in both the nature of your hike and the trail you tromp. East or west, however, most of the trails are similar in one respect: They are generally shorter than hikes you might consider in other forests of Oregon or Washington. Although you can extend almost any hike in this book by climbing farther or spending more time afield, it is the nature of Gorge geography and demography that limits trail length.

In the wet western end, where the Columbia River spreads its arms to welcome the Pacific, you'll walk rain-forest pathways and often wonder if the fog or drizzle would let up long enough to allow you to admire the view upriver. As you move upriver, however, the forest begins to dry and evergreens turn from cedar and fir to pine, and Oregon white oak replaces alder and maple. Trails here alternate between soft leaf-covered dirt to lumpy, sharp basalt paths that are more comfortably negotiated with a sturdy pair of hiking boots. The difference between the east and west ends of the Gorge is most noticeable in a 15-mile stretch between Hood River and The Dalles. One minute, you're hiking the forested hill to Mitchell Point (see hike #21) and the next you're exploring the sage and basalt of the Columbia River Highway Trail (see hike #25). Note that in this book the driveable parts of the highway are referred to as Historic Columbia River Highway 30, while the hikeable parts of the trail are called Historic Columbia River Highway, or the old Columbia River Highway Trail.

Noticeable, but not quite so dramatic, is the difference between the Oregon and the Washington sides of the Gorge. Oregon's side faces north and is generally steeper, wetter, and colder. Washington's side faces south, with rolling hills and high meadows that warm quicker in the spring and turn to gold faster in the fall. For the day hiker, it may mean the difference between slogging in cold drizzle or crossing the river to warmer and perhaps drier pathways. As experienced day hikers in Portland and Vancouver know, if it's raining in the city, it's likely to be sunny by the time they reach White Salmon or Hood River.

Another difference day hikers might notice between the Gorge and other hiking areas is the often confusing number of land managers in the Gorge. When the Columbia River Gorge National Scenic Area was born in 1986, administrators from the U.S. Forest Service, Oregon and Washington states, and six counties were asked to manage it together. Although two decades have passed, you may notice a few organizational bugs still to be worked out; for instance, there's a confusing array of permits and passes, and trail signs range from hand-carved placards to concrete-and-metal posts that occasionally face the wrong direction.

Finally, almost all of the trails in the Columbia Gorge can be hiked throughout the year. Severe winters are rare in the Gorge, but when one strikes, snowdrifts can sulk on some trails through March. Most years, the pathways along the river can be hiked year-round. Some of the trails popular in the summer might be more enjoyable for locals or visitors in late fall or winter, simply for the relative solitude. When Mother Nature starts spitting snow and freezing rain, however, stay away from steep or rocky routes and stick to lowland walks to awesome waterfalls. A good guideline to remember: If it's snowing in Portland or Vancouver, it's going to get worse upriver.

Now, hit the trail and try to picture Lewis and Clark walking alongside—and enjoying it.

1. Rooster Rock Loop

RATING	
DISTANCE	3.0 miles round-trip
HIKING TIME	1 hour
ELEVATION GAIN	120 feet
HIGH POINT	160 feet
DIFFICULTY LEVEL	Easy
BEST SEASON	Fall, winter
PERMITS/CONTACT	Day-use permit required/Rooster Rock State Park, (503) 695-2261 or (800) 551-6949
MAPS	USGS Bridal Veil; Green Trails Bridal Veil 428
TRAIL NOTES	Leashed dogs okay; kid-friendly

The Hike

Here's a fine family walk, suitable for youngsters of all ages. The fall forest is a great place for collecting leaves the color of Halloween.

Getting There

From Portland, drive east on Interstate 84 for about 22 miles to Exit 25 and follow signs to the park entrance. The trailhead is located at the east end of the easternmost parking area, 80 feet above sea level.

The Columbia River stretches east from the Rooster Rock overlook.

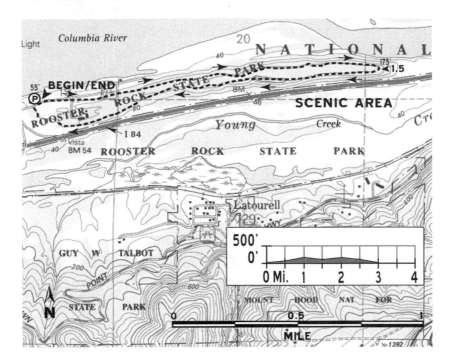

The Trail

Portland proximity, a great riverfront beach, and sunny days lure bathers—both suited and birthday-suited—to Rooster Rock State Park in flocks on warm spring and summer days. Simply finding a parking spot on one of these days could be a problem, so if you plan a family walk, wait until fall or winter.

Find the trail by climbing the low hill at the east end of the parking area, passing a restroom and bath house. A sign at the trailhead asks you to make certain Fido is on his leash. The trail meanders through a forest of maple, alder, and oak, just below a forested ridge that helps diminish the noise of westbound traffic on I-84. You'll get peekaboo glimpses of the Columbia River through the trees and walk on a colorful carpet of fallen leaves.

At **1.5** miles, you'll climb to the top of the ridge and look down a gently sloping, grassy meadow to the best view upriver. Here the trail loops back to the west along the crest of the ridge, and those seeking some respite from traffic noise may wish to return along the lower trail.

2. Latourell Falls Loop

RATING	🚶🚶🚶
DISTANCE	2.2 miles round-trip
HIKING TIME	1.5 hours
ELEVATION GAIN	535 feet
HIGH POINT	660 feet
DIFFICULTY LEVEL	Moderate
BEST SEASON	Spring
PERMITS/CONTACT	None/Guy W. Talbot State Park, (503) 695-2261 or (800) 551-6949
MAPS	USGS Bridal Veil; Green Trails Bridal Veil 428
TRAIL NOTES	Leashed dogs okay; kid-friendly

The Hike

It's a moderate climb up a forested hillside into a mossy canyon to a waterfall with a surprise: It grows a second tier when hikers start back down the trail.

Upper Latourell Falls from above shows its second tier.

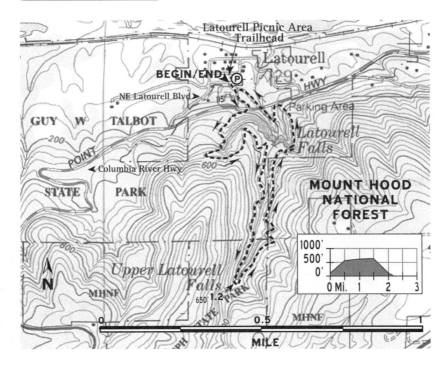

Getting There

From Portland, take Interstate 84 about 25 miles east to Exit 28 and follow the exit to the Historic Columbia River Highway 30. Turn right, or west, and follow the highway for about 3 miles, passing Bridal Veil and Latourell Falls parking areas. Take a hard right on NE Latourell Boulevard and follow it downhill to Guy W. Talbot State Park picnic area on the right. The trailhead is located uphill from the picnic area, 115 feet above sea level.

The Trail

Begin by climbing uphill on a paved trail along the eastern side of the picnic area, switching back and crossing the Historic Columbia River Highway west of the Latourell Creek bridge and Latourell Falls parking area. The parking area offers alternate trailhead parking, but the picnic area is quieter, has potable water, and is generally less crowded.

Cross the highway to the west and look for the trail as it climbs into the maple forest. The trail meanders uphill to the west before switching back and traversing into the forested gorge above the Lower Latourell Falls, 0.4 mile from the trailhead. You'll climb right, passing a trail that branches to the left and drops to a viewpoint of the lower falls—don't worry, you'll get a more spectacular view on your return. Continue climbing, never far from the sound or sight of Latourell Creek, as you traverse the emerald canyonside.

You'll arrive at a footbridge 1.2 miles from the trailhead that crosses Latourell Creek just below the wide pool formed at the base of Upper Latourell Falls, which appear to spout from the cliff as if from a fire nozzle and plunge about 100 feet into a pool. The footbridge provides an excellent view of the falls, but cross the bridge and follow the trail as it climbs back along the opposite side of the canyon. Now turn around and look back to see the *upper* Upper Latourell Falls, hidden from view at the bridge.

Now the route begins to drop along the east ridge bordering the creek to a junction with the lower falls trail, 1.9 miles from the trailhead. Stay right and descend to a paved viewing platform at the lower falls, which are higher—249 feet—and by virtue of their proximity to the Columbia Highway, draw more tourists.

To return to Guy W. Talbot State Park, turn left and follow the paved trail as it switches back under the highway bridge at the base of the lower falls and crosses Latourell Creek to emerge at the picnic area.

Upper Latourell Falls from below hides its second tier.

3. Angel's Rest

RATING	🚶🚶🚶🚶
DISTANCE	4.4 miles round-trip
HIKING TIME	3 hours
ELEVATION GAIN	1,540 feet
HIGH POINT	1,640 feet
DIFFICULTY LEVEL	Moderately difficult
BEST SEASON	Fall, early summer
PERMITS/CONTACT	None/Columbia River Gorge National Scenic Area, (541) 308-1700
MAPS	USGS Bridal Veil; Green Trails Bridal Veil 428
TRAIL NOTES	Leashed dogs okay

The Hike

The path to Angel's Rest is steep in places but worth the climb to the most spectacular trailside viewpoint in the lower Columbia Gorge.

Getting There

Take Interstate 84 about 25 miles east from Portland and take Exit 28 to the Historic Columbia River Highway 30. The parking area for the Angel's Rest Trail No. 415 is on the right, 100 feet above sea level; a quieter overflow parking lot is just west on the Columbia River Highway, uphill to the left, 150 feet above sea level.

The Trail

The hike to Angel's Rest begins on a forested hillside, climbing to the east and crossing a rocky slope where the tread is paved by sharp clods of basalt. Hikers in tennis shoes might wish they'd worn more protective trail shoes. You'll round a ridge above the Coopey Creek Gorge and hear Coopey Falls below the trail to the left. Here the trail contours down to a bridge crossing Coopey Creek, **0.7** mile from the trailhead. The creek furnishes the only water for hikers with filter bottles or pumps in midsummer.

The trail then begins to climb the ridge above Coopey Creek, switching back to a viewpoint overlooking the Columbia River Gorge, **1.4** miles from the trailhead. You can look up to see the

The view upriver from Angel's Rest.

burned bluff below Angel's Rest. The route heads upward in switchbacks along a trail that looks as if it would be slippery clay on rainy days. You'll emerge on the brushy hillside scarred by a 1991 fire.

The view grows increasingly wide as you continue climbing in switchbacks, turning to the south and traversing a field of flat rocks. A final switchback leads to a trail junction, with Angel's Rest a short scramble to the left, 2.2 miles from the trailhead. Angel's Rest is an airy perch with eyeball-melting views up and down the Columbia River; hikers with an irrational fear of heights—like me—may be more comfortable below. The summit of Mount Adams is visible to the east-northeast on clear days.

Going Farther

For an excellent view of Angel's Rest and a more sheltered picnic spot on windy or rainy days, continue to the right past the way

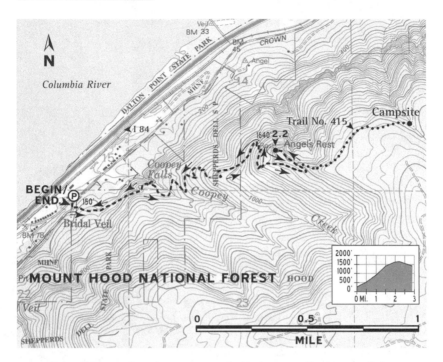

trail leading to the viewpoint and climb **0.1** mile to a trail junction. A small sign on the right may point to "Fox Glove Way," and Devil's Rest, but you'll turn left on Angel's Rest Trail No. 415 and walk for another **0.5** mile through a splendid old forest to a shaded campsite and tiny creek. Round-trip from this turnaround point is **5.8** miles.

4. Wahkeena Falls Loop

RATING	🚶🚶🚶🚶🚶
DISTANCE	5.8 miles round-trip
HIKING TIME	3.5 hours
ELEVATION GAIN	1,525 feet
HIGH POINT	1,600 feet
DIFFICULTY LEVEL	Moderately difficult
BEST SEASON	Spring, fall
PERMITS/CONTACT	None/Columbia River Gorge National Scenic Area, (541) 308-1700
MAPS	USGS Multnomah Falls; Green Trails Bridal Veil 428
TRAIL NOTES	Leashed dogs okay

The Hike

The climb up the forested canyon from Wahkeena Falls offers a less-crowded, beautiful alternative for viewing Multnomah Falls, the highest and most popular tourist location in the Columbia Gorge.

Multnomah Falls never fails to draw a crowd.

Getting There

From Portland, take Interstate 84 about 25 miles to Bridal Veil, Exit 28. Take the exit and drive to its junction with the Historic Columbia River Highway 30 and turn east, or left. Drive 2.5 miles to the Wahkeena Falls Trail No. 442 trailhead at the Wahkeena Falls parking area, 75 feet above sea level.

The Trail

On April 14, 1806, Meriwether Lewis wrote of this region: "Some handsome cascades are seen on either hand tumbling from the stupendous rocks of the mountain into the river." If you're unlucky enough to be limited to one or two hikes in the Columbia Gorge, choose this walk. You'll know you've gotten a workout, and you'll wander splendid forest and visit the Big Kahuna of waterfalls while enjoying relative solitude on most of the hike.

Fairy Falls is one of the lesser cascades on the Wahkeena Falls Loop hike.

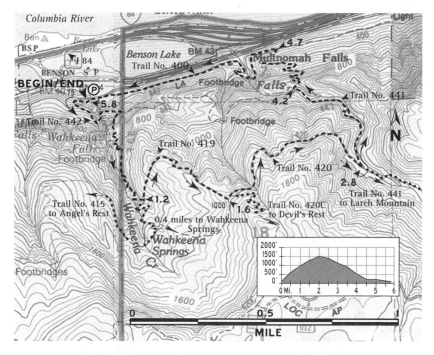

A tip: Carry plenty of film or digital storage plus a wide-angle lens for the camera. Without it, you'll have to back up all the way to Seattle to get all 630 feet of upper and lower Multnomah Falls in the obligatory snapshot.

From the parking area below Wahkeena Falls or alternate parking in the picnic area below, climb the paved Wahkeena Falls Trail as it ascends the ridge above the west side of the falls. It switches back at **0.2** mile and crosses Wahkeena Creek at a viewpoint below the falls—242 feet high—where the paved trail ends.

Continue climbing for 0.8 mile in a dozen switchbacks, past a viewpoint at **0.4** mile, to 30-foot Fairy Falls and a junction with Trail No. 419 at **1.2** miles from the trailhead (419 C on Friends of Multnomah Falls handout maps). This is a good turnaround spot for families with younger children.

To continue, climb Trail No. 419 to the left in more switchbacks. You'll round a fir-forested ridge and a side trail to a viewpoint and pass areas burned by a 1991 wildfire. At **1.6** miles from the trailhead, reach a junction with Trail No. 410. This is a confusing

Wahkeena Falls is the first awesome waterfall you'll encounter on the hike past Multnomah Falls.

junction because a sign indicates "To Columbia River Highway 1.9 miles" and points to the right fork of the trail. Don't take it.

Instead, stay left and walk 100 feet to a second junction with the Devil's Rest Trail No. 420C. Stay left at this junction and continue on Trail No. 420 as it contours through forest and burned areas with views to the Columbia below. After 0.8 mile, you'll round a ridge above Multnomah Creek and drop in switchbacks 0.4 mile to a junction with the Larch Mountain Trail No. 441, just below Upper Multnomah Falls, at 2.8 miles from the trailhead.

Turn left at this junction and walk beside the creek on trail blasted from volcanic rock, at one point along a rock wall as the trail passes underneath an overhanging cliff. The trail continues to descend along the creek, passing Ecola and Welsendanger Falls

Rockwork along Multnomah Creek mimics the early work beside the Columbia River Highway.

before crossing Multnomah Creek, **4.2** miles from the trailhead. The path is paved from this point as it climbs to a viewpoint overlooking Multnomah Falls, just across the bridge to the left. It's 0.2 mile to the viewpoint and here is where you can expect to encounter the first Multnomah tourist crowds.

Stay right from the junction with the viewpoint trail as the paved path climbs out of the gorge, then drops in switchbacks for 0.5 mile to a junction with the Columbia Gorge Trail No. 400 at **4.7** miles. Turn left and continue down to Multnomah Falls Lodge, crossing the Benson Bridge. To return to the Wahkeena Falls parking area, walk west in front of the lodge to the west end of the parking lot to find a trail marked "Return Trail 442" and follow it as it parallels Highway 30 for 0.6 mile.

5. Gorge Trail No. 400, Triple Falls

RATING	𝄕 𝄕 𝄕 𝄕
DISTANCE	5.2 miles
HIKING TIME	3 hours
ELEVATION GAIN	710 feet
HIGH POINT	760 feet
DIFFICULTY LEVEL	Moderately difficult
BEST SEASON	Spring, fall
PERMITS/CONTACT	Day-use permit required/Ainsworth State Park, (800) 551-6949
MAPS	USGS Multnomah Falls; Green Trails Bridal Veil 428
TRAIL NOTES	Leashed dogs okay; kid-friendly

The Hike

The hike to Oneonta Gorge from Ainsworth State Park provides a less-crowded alternative for woodland pedestrians to view some awesome waterfalls.

Hikers can wade up the narrow canyon of Oneonta Gorge after trekking the Gorge Trail No. 400, Triple Falls.

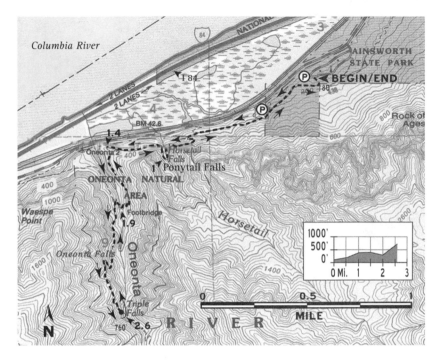

Getting There

Take Interstate 84 about 32 miles from Portland to Ainsworth, Exit 35, and follow the signs to the Ainsworth State Park Campground. The trailhead begins at the west end of the campground loop, 150 feet above sea level; or travel 0.5 mile farther west on the Historic Columbia River Highway 30 at the Ainsworth Picnic Area, 80 feet above sea level.

The Trail

The Columbia Gorge Trail stretches in bits and pieces for about 35 miles up the river, generally following the route of the Columbia River Highway. This section is likely the first you'll encounter as you explore the trails of the Columbia Gorge.

The hike has several trailheads, but the route from Ainsworth State Park Campground is especially convenient to those who are spending a weekend and camping at the park. From the campground, the trail climbs past an old well site and joins the Gorge Trail No. 400 **0.2** mile from the trailhead. Turn right and follow Gorge Trail No. 400 as it drops to a junction with the trail leading down to the Ainsworth Picnic Area, **0.4** mile from the trailhead.

The Gorge Trail No. 400, Triple Falls, passes behind Ponytail Falls.

Stay left here and begin a mile-long traverse in forest above I-84 and the quieter Columbia River Highway. After passing above Horsetail Falls, **0.8** mile from the trailhead, you'll arrive at a junction with a trail climbing up from the falls. Stay left again and traverse above Horsetail Creek to a view of Ponytail Falls. This view is unique, since the trail passes behind the falls before it begins to climb out of the canyon and traverse once again above the highway.

At **1.4** miles, you'll see a trail winding downhill to the Oneonta trailhead; turn left to begin an ascending traverse above the steep-walled Oneonta Gorge, crossing the gorge on a high bridge **1.9** miles from the trailhead. Just beyond, you'll climb the hillside to a junction with the Triple Falls Trail No. 424. Turn left on this trail and climb along the Oneonta Gorge for 0.7 mile to a turnaround viewpoint at Triple Falls at **2.6** miles, an awesome waterfall if ever there was one.

Going Farther

Although not a trail, the hike up Oneonta Gorge is a grand adventure, especially on a hot midsummer day. It makes a good way to cool off after the Triple Falls hike. On your return, cross the bridge over Oneonta Gorge and stay left at the trail junction, dropping steeply to the parking area on the Columbia River Highway. You

The view down Horsetail Creek from behind Ponytail
Falls provides an unusual perspective.

can also return to the Ainsworth trailhead and drive 2 miles west
on the Columbia River Highway to the Oneonta parking areas on
either side of the creek.

You'll be wading up the creekbed itself, past basalt walls of
Oneonta Gorge, where several unique native plants grow. The canyon
stretches about 0.3 mile upstream to Oneonta Falls, with the last
0.1 mile through water that can reach your thighs.

6. Larch Mountain Loop

RATING	🚶🚶🚶🚶
DISTANCE	5.7 miles round-trip
HIKING TIME	3 hours
ELEVATION GAIN	1,300 feet
HIGH POINT	3,950 feet
DIFFICULTY LEVEL	Moderately difficult
BEST SEASON	Fall
PERMITS/CONTACT	None/Columbia River Gorge National Scenic Area, (541) 308-1700
MAPS	USGS Bridal Veil; Green Trails Bridal Veil 428
TRAIL NOTES	Leashed dogs okay; kid-friendly

The Hike

Try this walk if you'd like a Columbia Gorge hike that is unique: Both the best view and the downhill portion of the path can be found at the trailhead.

Mount Hood is but one of the Cascade snow giants that can be seen from Sherrard Point, the trailhead for the Larch Mountain Loop.

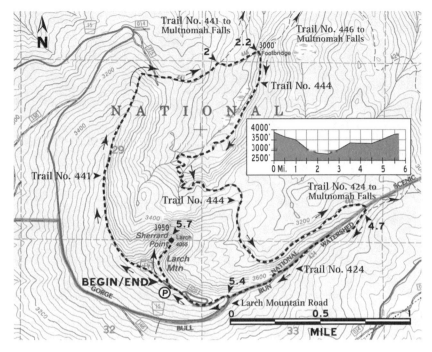

Getting There

From Portland, follow Interstate 84 about 25 miles to Exit 22, turn right and follow NE Corbett Hill Road 1.5 miles to its junction with the Historic Columbia River Highway 30. Turn left and follow Highway 30 1.9 miles to the Larch Mountain Road. Turn right and take the Larch Mountain Road 14 miles to the parking area and trailhead, 3,950 feet above sea level.

The Trail

Sherrard Point, a quarter-mile over or around the 4,056-foot-high Larch Mountain summit on a paved trail, is a spectacular viewpoint where you'll want to linger before or after your hike. You can see five snow giants: Rainier, Adams, St. Helens, Hood, and Jefferson, as well as the green and blue stretch of the Columbia River Valley. In fact, the hike isn't nearly as lustrous as the view from Sherrard Point. So plan to take this walk before lunch and picnic there.

Begin by following Multnomah Creek Trail No. 441 at the southwestern end of the parking area past a picnic area. Follow it downhill through an evergreen forest on a gentle grade along the crest of a wide ridge.

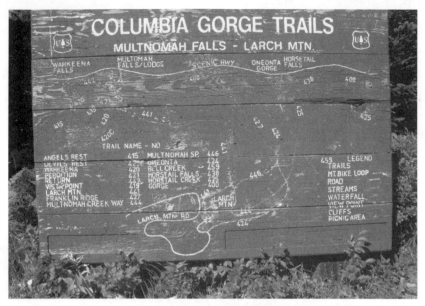

A sign at the Larch Mountain trailhead maps the
routes of the Columbia Gorge.

About **1.5** miles from the trailhead, you'll cross a closed gravel road and drop into the forest again to a junction with Trail No. 444, **2.0** miles from the trailhead. Follow Trail No. 444 to the right to a footlog crossing Multnomah Creek, **2.2** miles from trailhead, and a junction with Trail No. 446. This is the low point of your hike, about 2,780 feet above sea level. It's uphill from here, but you'll find only a few short sections that younger children and tired old hikers like me might describe as "steep."

Climb along a wet meadow beside Multnomah Creek, where summer coaxes shooting star and marsh marigold into bloom. This area can get buggy in summer; best wait until the mosquito squadrons head for their hangars after the first frost. At about **3.0** miles, you'll climb in switchbacks away from the creek, cross a broad ridge under Sherrard Point, and contour around the headwaters of Oneonta Creek. Continue climbing to a junction with Trail No. 424, **4.7** miles from the trailhead.

Turn right on Trail No. 424 and follow it as it climbs to Larch Mountain Road at **5.4** miles, 0.3 mile below the Larch Mountain parking area. Walk the road or climb to an overflow parking lot to the right to close the loop.

7. Wauna Viewpoint

RATING	🚶🚶🚶
DISTANCE	3.6 miles round-trip
HIKING TIME	2 hours
ELEVATION GAIN	980 feet
HIGH POINT	1,100 feet
DIFFICULTY LEVEL	Moderately difficult
BEST SEASON	Fall
PERMITS/CONTACT	Northwest Forest Pass required/ Columbia River Gorge National Scenic Area, (541) 308-1700
MAPS	USGS Bonneville Dam; Green Trails Bonneville Dam 429
TRAIL NOTES	Leashed dogs okay; kid-friendly

The Hike

Enjoy this moderate climb to a spectacular Gorge viewpoint, courtesy of those blokes who provide electricity from Bonneville Dam.

Getting There

Follow Interstate 84 from Portland about 44 miles to Eagle Creek Recreation Area, Exit 41. Turn right at the stop sign and drive to a picnic area and trailhead along Eagle Creek, 120 feet above sea level.

The climb to the Wauna Viewpoint crosses Eagle Creek.

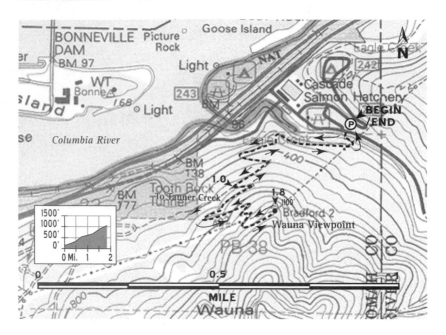

The Trail

You'll have company on this hike pretty much year-round, but in fall the crowds thin out a bit. In addition to solitude, a fall hike in the Eagle Creek area lets you get up close and personal with returning spawning coho and king salmon.

Begin by crossing the cable bridge across from the picnic area, a great spot for watching the salmon in the creek below. Take the right fork of the trail at the west end of the bridge and switchback a couple of times. You'll gain elevation and begin a climbing traverse through a steep hillside forest where you can get peekaboo views of the Eagle Creek picnic area below. The trail heads uphill on a gentle grade, rounding a ridge to an overlook with a view of Bonneville Dam and the freeway.

Beyond, the trail climbs gently again in switchbacks past views through the trees to the Columbia below. At 1.0 mile, you'll arrive at a junction marked by a historic mileage sign. Turn left here and begin a steeper series of switchbacks through open forest for 0.8 mile to rocks and an overlook at the base of a power line tower at 1.8 miles. Look upriver to Bridge of the Gods and downriver toward Beacon Rock and—if you squint really hard—the bartender at McMenamin's in Troutdale. Okay, maybe not that far.

8. Gorge Trail No. 400, Eagle Creek– Tanner Creek

RATING	🥾🥾
DISTANCE	4.2 miles round-trip
HIKING TIME	2 hours
ELEVATION GAIN	1,200 feet
HIGH POINT	720 feet
DIFFICULTY LEVEL	Moderate
BEST SEASON	Fall
PERMITS/CONTACT	Northwest Forest Pass required/ Columbia River Gorge National Scenic Area, (541) 308-1700
MAPS	USGS Bonneville Dam; Green Trails Bonneville Dam 429
TRAIL NOTES	Leashed dogs okay; kid-friendly

The Hike

This is a good walk for those seeking exercise on a gloomy-weather day when views aren't important. You'll get a chance to watch spawning salmon at Eagle Creek.

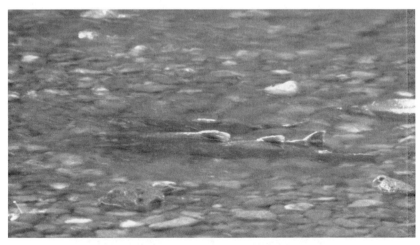

Salmon spawn in Eagle Creek during fall and spring, next to Gorge Trail No. 400 access.

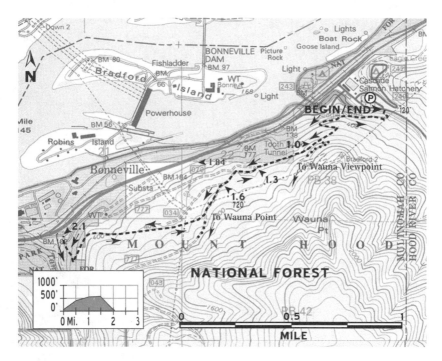

Getting There

From Portland, follow Interstate 84 about 44 miles to Eagle Creek Recreation Area, Exit 41. Turn right at the stop sign and drive to a picnic area and trailhead along Eagle Creek, 120 feet above sea level.

The Trail

The first mile of this hike follows the route to Wauna Viewpoint (see hike #7). Begin by crossing the cable bridge over Eagle Creek, a great spot for viewing spawning salmon. Turn right at the junction at the west end of the bridge and begin climbing in switchbacks to a hillside traverse above Eagle Creek. You'll round a ridge at an overlook and in three switchbacks, climb to a junction with the Wauna Viewpoint Trail.

The junction, 1.0 mile from the trailhead, is marked by an old stone Columbia Gorge Trail mileage sign. Stay right here and continue to traverse along the hillside above the river, never straying from the sound of the interstate highway below.

At 1.3 miles, the trail intersects an old roadbed at a switchback. Stay left on the road as it climbs gently for 0.3 mile to a second

Table Mountain dusted with early autumn snow is visible across the
Columbia River from Gorge Trail No. 400.

intersection with the trail at **1.6** miles. Follow the trail to the right
as it begins a 600-foot, 0.5-mile descent to the trailhead and turnaround point at Tanner Creek at **2.1** miles from the trailhead.

Going Farther

Hikers seeking a little more exercise or a visit to nearby waterfalls
can combine this hike with the Wahclella Falls Loop (see hike #12),
which begins at the turnaround point. It's a 2-mile hike, round-trip,
to the falls.

9. Ruckel Creek Trail No. 405

RATING	🥾🥾🥾
DISTANCE	9.8 miles round-trip
HIKING TIME	6 hours
ELEVATION GAIN	3,640 feet
HIGH POINT	3,760 feet
DIFFICULTY LEVEL	Difficult
BEST SEASON	Summer
PERMITS/CONTACT	Northwest Forest Pass required/ Columbia River Gorge National Scenic Area, (541) 308-1700
MAPS	USGS Bonneville Dam; Green Trails Bonneville Dam 429
TRAIL NOTES	Leashed dogs okay; bikes allowed about 1 mile

The Hike

Here's a long, tough climb into some of the wildest areas of the country surrounding the Columbia River Gorge. You'll hike through splendid old forest and across wildflower-packed meadows to the edge of 4,000-foot-high Benson Plateau.

Getting There

Follow Interstate 84 about 44 miles from Portland to Eagle Creek Recreation Area, Exit 41. Turn right at the stop sign and drive to a picnic area and trailhead along Eagle Creek, 120 feet above sea level.

Hikers descend the steep Ruckel Creek Trail No. 405.

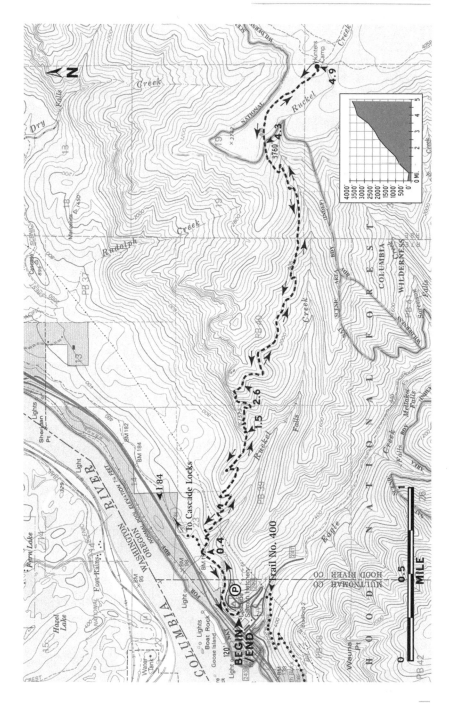

The Trail

You could wander around the Eagle Creek Recreation Area and Campground for fifteen minutes, trying to find the trailhead. The best way is to walk north from the picnic parking area past the buildings on your right to a paved bicycle trail that turns east beside I-84.

The paved trail parallels I-84 for several hundred feet before arcing to the south below the Eagle Creek Campground and joining Columbia Gorge Trail No. 400. Hike through flat meadow and open forest with interpretive signs and markers on the pavement. This portion of the route is good for in-line skaters, bicyclists, or families with young children.

After 0.4 mile, you'll cross chattering Ruckel Creek and immediately arrive at the junction with Ruckel Creek Trail No. 405. Turn right and begin climbing immediately in switchbacks above the creek canyon. The trail uphill gives neither quarter nor rest. Just before crossing underneath power lines, you'll pass the remains of ceremonial rock pits constructed by Native Americans centuries ago.

The route switches back along the nose of a forested ridge for 1.5 miles. Just when you catch your breath, you'll begin another series of steeper, shorter switchbacks. The trail gains nearly 800 feet in the next 0.7 mile before it levels off—relatively speaking at 2.6 miles. From here, it climbs gently for more than a mile through forest and hillside meadows, where you risk being buried by a wildflower avalanche in the summer. Just as you begin to approach Ruckel Creek, the trail switches back again and climbs the canyonside in steep gulps. The creek rushes raucously below and the trail here looks as if it could get slippery in wet weather.

A pleasant surprise awaits about 4.3 miles from the trailhead: the final 0.6-mile section of the path that might actually be described as gentle. This is the northerly edge of the Benson Plateau, and at 4.9 miles, you'll see a campsite and trail junction—your turnaround point.

Going Farther

Strong hikers accustomed to scrambling and route-finding can return to the trailhead via an unmaintained path and extremely steep scramble that crosses Ruckel Creek and follows the west side of the canyon back to the Eagle Creek Campground. Don't take this route if you are uncomfortable on steep, rocky, exposed slopes.

10. Gorge Trail No. 400, Eagle Creek– Bridge of the Gods

RATING	
DISTANCE	4.4 miles round-trip
HIKING TIME	2 hours
ELEVATION GAIN	160 feet
HIGH POINT	240 feet
DIFFICULTY LEVEL	Easy
BEST SEASON	Winter
PERMITS/CONTACT	Northwest Forest Pass required/ Columbia River Gorge National Scenic Area, (541) 308-1700
MAPS	USGS Bonneville Dam; Green Trails Bonneville Dam 429
TRAIL NOTES	Leashed dogs okay; kid-friendly; bikes allowed

The Hike

Plan this easy walk for a rainy day when you'd like some outdoor exercise with your kids or dogs.

Getting There

Follow Interstate 84 about 44 miles from Portland to Eagle Creek Recreation Area, Exit 41. Turn right at the stop sign and drive to a picnic area and trailhead along Eagle Creek, 120 feet above sea level.

The Trail

To begin, walk north from the picnic parking area past buildings on your right to the paved bicycle trail that circles to the east and parallels I-84 for several hundred feet. The paved portion of the path continues for about a mile, never straying far from the interstate.

After passing a trail marker and memorial, the route joins with the Gorge Trail No. 400, which drops onto the paved trail from the Eagle Creek Campground above. At 0.4 mile from the trailhead, stay left at the junction with the Ruckel Creek Trail No. 405 and follow the pavement to its end. Families with young children might find this walk of about 2.5 miles round-trip to be enough. For a

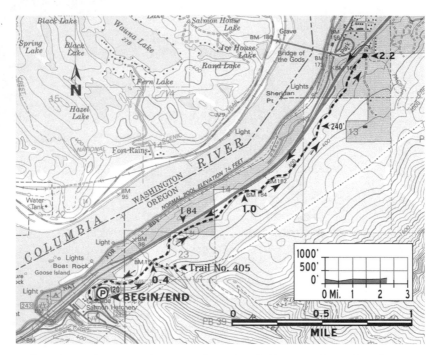

longer workout, continue on Gorge Trail No. 400 through a forest of maple and alder as it alternately climbs and drops gently.

At 2.2 miles from the trailhead, the path emerges onto the gravel extension of Moody Street on the outskirts of Cascade Locks. Just across the road, you'll find the winter trailhead for the Oregon section of the Pacific Crest Trail 2000—in case you'd like to get a bit more exercise and walk south to Mexico.

11. Gorge Trail No. 400, Tanner Creek– McCord Creek

RATING	🚶🚶
DISTANCE	6.0 miles round-trip
HIKING TIME	3 hours
ELEVATION GAIN	160 feet
HIGH POINT	240 feet
DIFFICULTY LEVEL	Easy
BEST SEASON	Winter
PERMITS/CONTACT	Northwest Forest Pass required/ Columbia River Gorge National Scenic Area, (541) 308-1700
MAPS	USGS Bonneville Dam; Green Trails Bonneville Dam 429
TRAIL NOTES	Leashed dogs okay; kid-friendly

The Hike

Here's another walk through a leafy forest best saved for a day when the only views might be of your muddy boots on the trail or of woodland mist in the distance.

Getting There

Follow Interstate 84 from Portland about 42 miles to Exit 40. Take Exit 40 and turn right at the stop sign. Turn left at a T junction to the parking area and Gorge Trail No. 400 trailhead, 120 feet above sea level.

The Trail

The Gorge Trail No. 400 is easily one of the most convenient ways to enjoy the great outdoors without straying from civilization. In fewer than forty minutes from the Portland airport, you can grab a memory of hiking the emerald Northwest and still make that afternoon meeting. You won't be walking in the wilderness–what with an interstate highway next door–but that's a small price if you're trying to get some exercise outdoors on a rainy day.

Begin by crossing the bridge over Tanner Creek and climbing to a switchback to the north. You'll circle a broad ridge about 160 feet above the eastbound lanes of the interstate. The trail contours

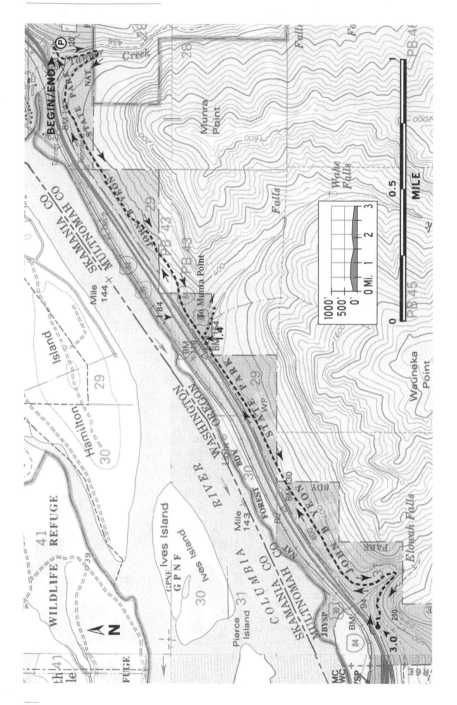

through maple and alder forest, alternately climbing and dropping in gentle grades. At **1.4** miles, you'll arrive at the junction with an unsigned way trail that climbs steeply to Munra Point.

Stay to the right and continue to traverse the forested John B. Yeon State Park above the interstate. You'll cross several rocky hillsides with views of the Columbia River and Ives Island. About **2.6** miles from the trailhead, you'll swing to the south around a ridge and enter the McCord Creek Canyon. Traverse the hillside to a crossing of the creek below Elowah Falls, climb out of the canyon, and descend in switchbacks to the turnaround point at the Elowah Falls trailhead at **3.0** miles.

Going Farther

For a view of Elowah Falls, climb in switchbacks less than 0.5 mile up the Elowah Falls Trail, 560 feet above sea level. Descend the same trail. The way trail that climbs 1.3 miles and 1,700 vertical feet to Munra Point is extremely steep, brushy, and rocky. It should be attempted only by hikers with route-finding experience who are comfortable on exposed slopes—but the view from the top is one of the most rewarding in the lower Columbia Gorge.

12. Wahclella Falls Loop

RATING	
DISTANCE	2.0 miles round-trip
HIKING TIME	1 hour
ELEVATION GAIN	300 feet
HIGH POINT	380 feet
DIFFICULTY LEVEL	Moderate
BEST SEASON	Spring
PERMITS/CONTACT	Northwest Forest Pass required/ Columbia River Gorge National Scenic Area, (541) 308-1700
MAPS	USGS Tanner Butte; Green Trails Bonneville Dam 429
TRAIL NOTES	Leashed dogs okay; kid-friendly

The Hike

If viewing a spectacular waterfall at the end of a relatively short climb through lowland forests is on your agenda, this might be the best walk for you.

Trillium blossoms first in the western forests of the Gorge.

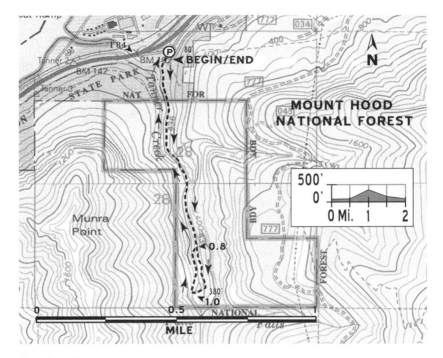

Getting There

Take Exit 40 off Interstate 84, about 42 miles from Portland. Turn right at the stop sign, stay right at a junction, and park in the paved lot at the trailhead, 120 feet above sea level.

The Trail

The route follows a closed dirt road upstream for about 0.2 mile along Tanner Creek. It passes a concrete dam, turns into a wide footpath, and crosses a tributary with its own 40-foot waterfall.

From here, climb in steps and water bars alongside Tanner Creek for about 0.5 mile. At **0.8** mile, you'll arrive at a junction of the short loop trail that climbs to a footbridge just below Wahclella Falls. Stay left and climb 0.2 mile to the bridge, a good spot for photos of the two-tiered falls. The first step plunges about 20 feet; the second, about 75.

When you've run out of digital storage or film, cross the bridge and follow the trail on the west bank past debris of a forty-year-old rock slide to cross Tanner Creek and close the loop.

13. Eagle Creek Trail No. 440

RATING	🚶🚶🚶🚶
DISTANCE	6.8 miles round-trip
HIKING TIME	3.5 hours
ELEVATION GAIN	640 feet
HIGH POINT	800 feet
DIFFICULTY LEVEL	Moderate
BEST SEASON	Fall, spring
PERMITS/CONTACT	Northwest Forest Pass required/ Columbia River Gorge National Scenic Area, (541) 308-1700
MAPS	USGS Bonneville Dam, USGS Tanner Butte; Green Trails Bonneville Dam 429
TRAIL NOTES	Leashed dogs okay

The Hike

This splendidly graded, wide path leads through old evergreen forest past spectacular waterfalls, clings to sheer cliffs, and crosses a deep canyon. It's one of the must-do hikes in the Gorge.

Getting There

Follow Interstate 84 about 44 miles from Portland to Eagle Creek Recreation Area, Exit 41. Turn right at the stop sign and drive past a picnic area along a one-lane road above Eagle Creek for 0.2 mile to the trailhead, 160 feet above sea level.

The Trail

On April 19, 1806, explorer Meriwether Lewis wrote of this region: "There was great joy with the natives last night in consequence of the arrival of the salmon; one of those fish was caught; this was the harbinger of good news to them. They informed us that these fish would arrive in great quantities in the course of about five days. This fish was dressed and being divided into small pieces [which] was given to each child in the village. This custom is founded in a superstitious opinion that it will hasten the arrival of the salmon."

The Eagle Creek Trail No. 440 might be called the footpath version of the Columbia River Highway, because it has nearly as

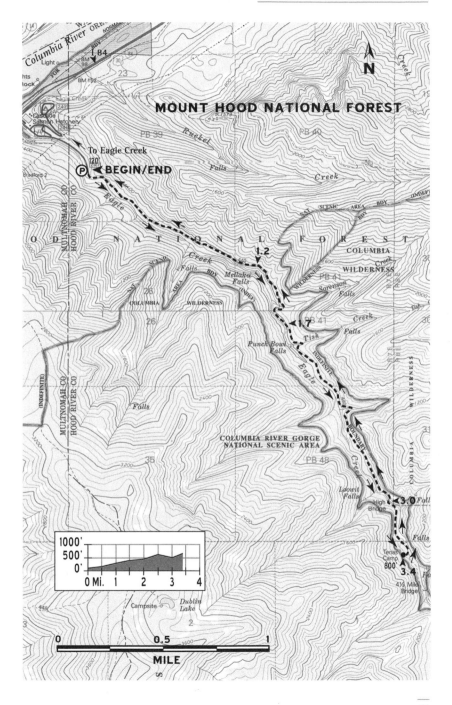

Eagle Creek carves a 100-foot-deep slot canyon in the basalt at High Bridge on the Eagle Creek Trail No. 440.

much history and is every bit as spectacular. At several points, it is carved from solid rock cliffs that plunge a hundred feet or more into the Eagle Creek canyon. So keep an eye on kids and leashes on pets. Fall is an excellent time for this hike if you'd like to watch spawning king and silver salmon. Spring might be best if you're a waterfall lover.

The trail climbs gently but steadily up the gorge carved by Eagle Creek. At **0.5** mile, it crosses the first of four cliffs above the creek on trails blasted out of basalt. The route never strays far from the Eagle Creek gorge, passing the Metlako Falls overlook, **1.2** miles from the trailhead. The falls, at least 100 feet high, were named for the Native American goddess of salmon by the Mazamas in 1915.

Continue beyond the overlook as the trail climbs into the Sorenson Creek canyon and crosses Sorenson Creek, a good source of water for hikers with filter bottles or pumps. You'll climb out of the canyon to an overlook trail leading to must-see Punch Bowl Falls, **1.7** miles from the trailhead.

Beyond, the trail crosses an unnamed creek on a high bridge before turning into the Eagle Creek gorge. Climb in forest along the steep hillside before turning along a final cliff crossing. Here, those who like me sometimes wet their pants when confronted

Some Columbia Gorge trails cross sheer cliffs, blasted out of solid rock.

by such exposure, will appreciate the steel cable strung along the inside of the cliff wall. I have calluses from gripping this safety line to this day.

You probably won't be so dramatically affected by the exposure and will calmly walk about 250 feet to a point where the trail turns and crosses High Bridge. This plank and metal span is about 100 feet above the narrow Eagle Creek gorge, 3.0 miles from the trailhead. Beyond, the trail turns upstream and contours to Tenas Camp, 3.4 miles from the trailhead. The campsite is a good turnaround spot, with creekside views of a waterfall and two inviting pools.

Going Farther

Eagle Creek Trail No. 440 continues upstream for another 3 miles on a gentle grade that invites hikers seeking a longer walk to spectacular 120-foot-high Tunnel Falls. Here the trail is blasted out of the rock and you'll pass behind the falls in a tunnel dynamited from basalt, about 60 feet up the cliff.

Tunnel Falls is 6.2 miles from the trailhead and makes a long day hike in spring or fall. If you make that your day-hiking goal, you might consider camping at Eagle Creek Campground at the trailhead. It's the nation's first Forest Service campground.

14. Pacific Crest Trail 2000, Cascade Locks—Dry Creek Falls

RATING	🚶🚶🚶
DISTANCE	4.4 miles round-trip
HIKING TIME	2 hours
ELEVATION GAIN	680 feet
HIGH POINT	880 feet
DIFFICULTY LEVEL	Moderate
BEST SEASON	Spring, fall
PERMITS/CONTACT	Northwest Forest Pass required/ Columbia River Gorge National Scenic Area, (541) 308-1700
MAPS	USGS Carson; Green Trails Bonneville Dam 429
TRAIL NOTES	Leashed dogs okay; kid-friendly

The Hike

This walk, good most any time of the year, is a fine springtime tune-up for hikers who spend their winters poring over maps and for families with young children.

Though Dry Creek lives up to its name in the fall, follow the trail upstream to Dry Creek Falls, which flows year-round.

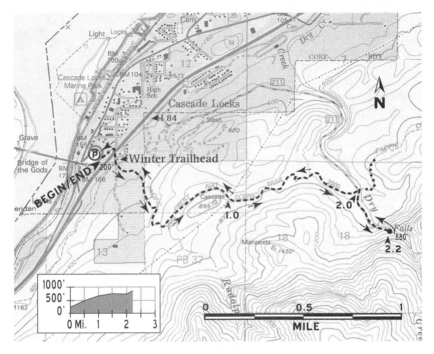

Getting There

From Portland, follow Interstate 84 to Cascade Locks, Exit 44. Drive
east 1.5 miles through Cascade Locks and turn left at the Bridge of
the Gods intersection. Follow the road as it loops toward the Bridge
of the Gods toll booth and look for a right turn into a rest area and
the Pacific Crest Trail (PCT). There is no sign indicating this parking area, but it is the official northern end of the Oregon section
of the PCT. The trailhead is located on the south side of the road
leading to the Bridge of the Gods, where a sign can be found, 200
feet above sea level.

Note: This trailhead is closed during winter. For the winter trailhead, continue east from the Bridge of the Gods intersection about
two blocks on WaNaPa Road to Moody Street, turn right and follow
Moody to the trailhead at its intersection with a gravel road just
underneath I-84, about 220 feet above sea level.

The Trail

One of the highlights of this hike is walking a trail that stretches
from Mexico to Canada. If you wait until late August or September,

there's a fair chance you'll cross paths with backpackers who began their trek in Mexico, way back in April.

The trail parallels I-84 for several hundred feet before intersecting a paved road at the Moody Street underpass at I-84. Follow the paved road uphill under I-84 and bear right on a gravel road for about 100 feet to the winter trailhead. The PCT takes off to the left; the Columbia Gorge No. 400 trailhead is on the right.

The trail climbs gently through alder and maple forest past a house before entering the forest and climbing in broad switchbacks to cross underneath a power line at 1.0 mile. Follow the dirt road under the power line uphill and look right just after the curve as the trail dives back into the forest.

At 1.1 miles, you'll crest a forested saddle and begin a gentle descent above a gully. The trail drops gently through the forest and emerges at a gravel road at Dry Creek, 2.0 miles from the trailhead. A footbridge crosses the creek here and makes a good picnic spot. Even in late fall, when Dry Creek lives up to its name, you'll hear the rush of water upstream of the bridge; follow the gravel road 0.2 mile uphill to 60-foot-high Dry Creek Falls, at 2.2 miles.

Going Farther

Hikers with two cars can make a 6.2-mile walk, one-way, from trailheads at Cascade Locks and Herman Creek Campground, east of Cascade Locks. Meet at Dry Creek Falls, and don't forget to trade car keys!

Mountain bike riders might enjoy the 2-mile ride to the falls along a dirt access road that starts just across WaNaPa Road from the entrance to Cascade Locks Marine Park. This road provides Cascade Locks city workers access to Dry Creek, part of the city watershed.

15. Herman Creek Pinnacles

RATING	🚶 🚶
DISTANCE	4.5 miles round-trip
HIKING TIME	2 hours
ELEVATION GAIN	640 feet
HIGH POINT	840 feet
DIFFICULTY LEVEL	Moderate
BEST SEASON	Fall, winter
PERMITS/CONTACT	Northwest Forest Pass required/ Columbia River Gorge National Scenic Area, (541) 308-1700
MAPS	USGS Carson; Green Trails Bonneville Dam 429
TRAIL NOTES	Leashed dogs okay; kid-friendly

The Hike

This forested walk makes a good fall or winter trek with the family, with a moderate climb for exercise and a longer key-exchange option.

Getting There

From Portland, take Interstate 84 east past Cascade Locks to Exit 47 and turn right on Herman Creek Road. Drive 0.5 mile west to the Herman Creek Recreation area and turn left, following signs to Herman Creek Campground. Turn right to the trailhead, 140 feet above sea level, just before the campground entrance.

The Trail

I planned to include several hikes in the Herman Creek area for the first edition of this book, but a wildfire in early July 2003 closed all of the trails. That is too bad, because the hikes around Herman Creek belong to the rare few walks in the Gorge where a day hiker can escape the noise of Interstate 84. I didn't know that until I returned to Herman Creek in the summer of 2010 to walk to the twin spires named the Herman Pinnacles.

The hike begins in a shady parking area where you'll find a restroom and picnic tables. The trail drops, then immediately begins climbing through the forest in wide switchbacks to cross a power

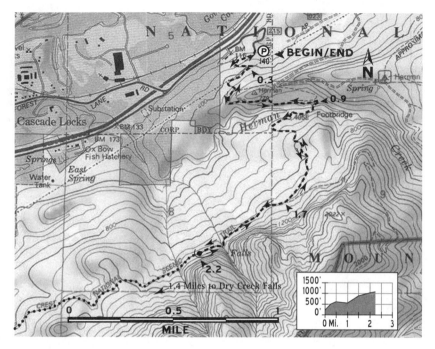

line and access road, **0.3** mile from the trailhead. The trail crosses the road near a switchback, and is marked with signs both going up and returning.

Once back in the forest of fir and maple, you'll swing south into the Herman Creek Canyon, climbing moderately for about a half-mile to a junction with the Herman Creek Trail (see hike #16). Turn right, round a shoulder, and begin to descend toward the creek through a rocky, open section of trail. As you pass, say a silent thanks to the Oregon Youth Conservation Corps workers who widened this section of the path in 2010.

The trail descends to a cool, shady steel footbridge across Herman Creek, **0.9** mile from the trailhead, then begins climbing more steeply up a wide ridge, passing through forest and basalt talus where you may be surprised to hear those micro hay farmers of alpine slopes—pikas—which populate some lower areas of the Gorge. The French word for "pika," by the way, is "pika." French for "pika on a stick" is "pika en brochette." I learned that by reading road signs and menus in Canada.

The trail climbs about 100 vertical feet in a little more than a half-mile before the grade eases, and at **1.7** miles, arrives at a junction with the Pacific Crest Trail 2000. Continue to the right on the PCT as the route contours southwesterly in forest and across wide rocky slopes to the base of an undernourished waterfall, 2.1 miles from the trailhead. The route continues another 0.1 mile to the Pinnacles, where a side trail leads to the base of the rocks.

Going Farther

Hikers looking for more exercise can continue on the PCT for another 1.4 miles to Dry Creek Falls (see hike #14). Those who have parked cars at the Cascade Locks and Herman Creek trailheads can make a one-way hike, exchanging keys at Dry Creek Falls or the Pinnacles. The distance between trailheads is 6.2 miles.

Traffic noise from Interstate 84 in the Herman Creek Campground is the least of any Oregon State Park campgrounds in the Gorge. If you're tent camping in the Gorge, Herman Creek is the spot for you.

The trail to Herman Pinnacles crosses Herman Creek on a steel bridge.

16. Herman Creek Trail

RATING	🚶🚶🚶🚶
DISTANCE	8 miles round-trip
HIKING TIME	4 hours
ELEVATION GAIN	1,500 feet
HIGH POINT	1,880 feet
DIFFICULTY LEVEL	Moderate
BEST SEASON	Summer
PERMITS/CONTACT	Northwest Forest Pass required/ Columbia River Gorge National Scenic Area, (541) 308-1700
MAPS	USGS Carson; Green Trails Bonneville Dam 429
TRAIL NOTES	Leashed dogs okay

The Hike

Here's a walk up a forested canyon beside one of the larger tributaries to the Columbia River, with a more difficult and longer loop trip option.

Getting There

From Portland, take Interstate 84 east past Cascade Locks to Exit 47 and turn right on Herman Creek Road. Drive 0.5 mile west to the Herman Creek Recreation area and turn left, following signs to Herman Creek Campground. Turn right to the trailhead, 140 feet above sea level, just before the campground entrance.

The Trail

The hike up the canyon carved by Herman Creek is reminiscent of the Eagle Creek Trail, minus all that extreme ledge walking along cliffs where death is imminent and your hands turn to raw hamburger while gripping the cable so you wont slip and tumble into the raging torrent below, and the sweat is pouring off you like a miniature Multnomah, and oh, God, why didn't you make me a golfer instead of a hiker so I wouldn't have to put up with this crap? Or maybe that's just me.

Anyway, the Herman Creek Trail is a bit like Eagle Creek, in that both head south, away from the noise of Interstate 84, and in a mile or so, all you can hear is the muffled shuffle of the creek below and the wind tickling the Oregon oak beside the path. The trail drops slightly before climbing in wide switchbacks and crossing a power line and access road near a switchback, 0.3 mile from the trailhead. The route re-enters the forest and continues to climb for about a half-mile to a trail junction with the Herman Bridge Trail 406E. Stay left here and climb more gently along a wide trail that was once an old road, reaching a saddle where you bid adieu to the sound of the interstate and the trail forks, 1.1 miles from the trailhead.

The left fork is Gorge Trail 400, the middle fork is Gorton Creek Trail 408, and the right fork is Herman Creek Trail 406. Stay right and continue southerly for another 0.1 mile to the junction with the Nick Eaton Trail 447, to the left. Your path is to the right, as the Herman Creek Trail 406 contours and climbs gently through the forest of evergreens and oak about 260 feet above the creek. The route climbs on an even grade for about another mile to a creek crossing just below a falls.

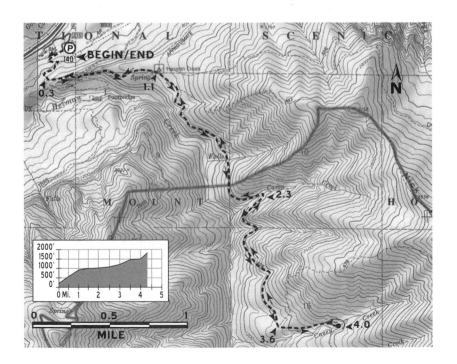

The lower portion of the Herman Creek Trail follows an old roadbed.

Beyond, round a wide ridge and climb into a steep canyon cut by Camp Creek, which splashes vigorously in the springtime, 2.3 miles from the trailhead. The path climbs out of the canyon and almost immediately turns into a smaller gorge, crosses it, and winds into a third gully before arcing south again and approaching a junction with the Casey Creek Trail 467, 3.6 miles from the trailhead. Stay right and continue another 0.4 mile to the crossing at Casey Creek, your turnaround point. The best spot for a picnic is at the campsite near the Casey Creek Trail junction.

Going Farther

For a strenuous 11.3-mile-loop hike involving a 3,000-foot elevation gain and loss, follow the Casey Creek Trail 467 uphill for 2
miles to the Nick Eaton Ridge Trail 447. Turn left and follow the
trail past two junctions, keeping left at both, heading downhill to
the junction with Herman Creek Trail, then turning right to meet
the trailhead.

The steep climb from the Herman Creek Trail up
Nick Eaton Ridge is a hiker-only path.

17. Mount Defiance (Hard Way)

RATING	🚶🚶🚶
DISTANCE	11.2 miles round-trip
HIKING TIME	8.5 hours
ELEVATION GAIN	4,900 feet
HIGH POINT	4,960 feet
DIFFICULTY LEVEL	Extreme
BEST SEASON	Summer
PERMITS/CONTACT	None/Columbia River Gorge National Scenic Area, (541) 308-1700
MAPS	USGS Mount Defiance; Green Trails Hood River 430
TRAIL NOTES	Leashed dogs okay

The Hike

This is a knee-punishing, lung-busting climb to one of the best views of the Columbia Gorge and the snowcapped giants bordering it, which by most hikers' accounts makes all that work worthwhile.

Getting There

From Portland, take Interstate 84 to Exit 54, a rest stop at Starvation Creek State Park, 60 feet above sea level. To return to Portland, you'll need to drive east on Interstate 84 to Exit 56 at Viento State Park.

The Trail

Three trails (and a four-wheel-drive access road) lead to this antenna-crowned peak overlooking the Columbia Gorge. Two of them, including the trail described here, are exceptionally difficult and will test the mettle of all but Real Mountain Climbers. And even they will still work up a sweat—the elevation gained on this trail is equivalent to starting at Timberline Lodge and climbing to the summit of Mount Hood. (The third route, known to the creaky-knees crowd, the exceptionally lazy, and perhaps a guidebook author or two, is very easy and covered in hike #18.)

So take a deep breath, stretch those muscles, and hit the trail with me. Begin by walking west toward the freeway exit on a sidewalk and trail along the opposite side of a Jersey barrier that separates

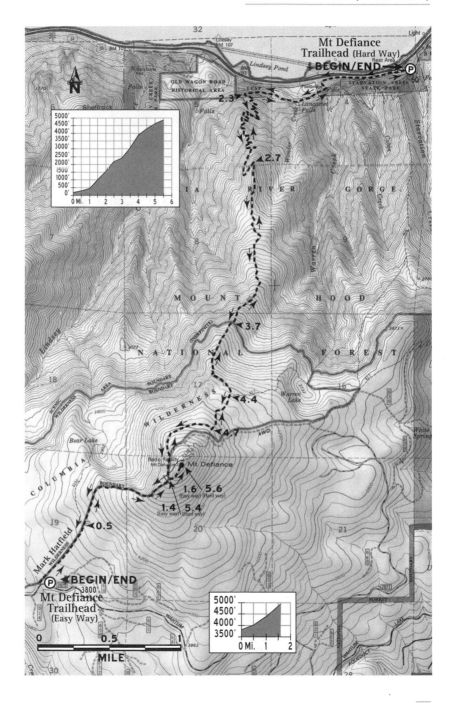

The upper portion of the Mount Defiance Trail traverses
a splendid rock garden.

you from interstate traffic. The trail drops away from the side of
the freeway into forest, and this level path is a good section to
warm up for the muscular torture to follow. You'll pass a junction
to the left with the Starvation Cutoff Trail at 0.3 mile from the
trailhead. Continue straight, passing Cabin Creek and Hole-in-the-
Wall falls, then turn and cross the bridge over Warren Creek. Just
beyond is a junction with the Starvation Ridge Trail; stay right
and climb on a moderate grade to a creek crossing below Lancaster Falls, 1.9 miles from the trailhead. This rather unimpressive
cascade honors Samuel Lancaster, the engineer who designed the
Historic Columbia River Highway.

Your path, Mount Defiance Trail 413, climbs into a power-line
clearing, and as it reaches the top, 2.3 miles from the trailhead, it
switches back and begins the steep and seemingly unending climb
up the forested ridge that divides Wonder and Warren creeks from
Lindsey Creek. I believe—but cannot prove beyond a reasonable
doubt—the crew that blazed this trail got tired of building switchbacks at No. 26, and simply turned directly up the ridge, 2.8 miles
from the trailhead.

You'll do the same if you want to stay on the trail, climbing
steeply through forest that provides few peekaboo views of the
creeks hundreds of yards below (which is as close to water as you'll
get on this hike). After another mile of climbing, you'll leave the

Columbia River Gorge National Scenic Area and enter the Columbia Wilderness, where the views open up a bit and bear grasses flash white plumes. If anything, the path gets steeper as you climb increasingly open slopes to a junction with the Warren Lake Trail 417, 4.4 miles from the trailhead. Stay right, here, and struggle another 0.3 mile up to a second junction. Take the right fork and begin a gentler contour to the west and southwest under the summit of Mount Defiance.

At 5.4 miles from the trailhead, you'll encounter a junction with the Mount Defiance Trail 413 (see hike #18). Stay left and climb the remaining 0.2 mile to the summit. High fives. Rehydrate. Enjoy the view of the Columbia Gorge and the snow giants to the south and north.

I would have rated this hike higher, except for the fact that the hiker must dodge cables and microwave dishes atop Mount Defiance, which detract from the feeling of getting away from it all. This is most disconcerting, I believe, for all of the hardy hikers who arrived here via the Hard Way.

18. Mount Defiance (Easy Way)

RATING	🚶🚶🚶
DISTANCE	3.2 miles round-trip
HIKING TIME	2 hours
ELEVATION GAIN	1,100 feet
HIGH POINT	4,960 feet
DIFFICULTY LEVEL	Easy
BEST SEASON	Summer
PERMITS/CONTACT	None/Mount Hood National Forest, (541) 352-6002
MAPS	USGS Mount Defiance
TRAIL NOTES	Leashed dogs okay; kid-friendly

The Hike

This is the short and easy route to one of the best views of the Columbia Gorge and Cascade peaks. (Refer to the map on page 55 for this trail.)

Getting There

From Portland, follow Interstate 84 to Hood River, Exit 62. Turn right and drive east to 13th Street. Turn right on 13th and drive uphill through the Hood River Heights business district as 13th merges into Tucker Road. Stay on Tucker as it makes three

The junction of the Hard and Easy ways up Mount Defiance is marked by this sign.

90-degree turns, the final being a left turn at Windmaster Corner. Continue following Tucker Road 8 miles to the Dee Highway intersection, then turn right past the old Dee mill, and right again on "Rainy Lake" road. Follow this road 0.3 mile to a junction with Green Road, and keep right on Punch Bowl Road for 1.1 miles to a three-way junction (and the end of the pavement). Take the left fork, Forest Road 2820, labeled "To Dead Point Road."

Drive 10.3 miles on Forest Road 2820 as it climbs toward the Rainy Lake Campground to a wide parking area on the left. The trailhead for Mount Defiance Trail No. 413 is across the road, 3,800 feet above sea level.

The top of the microwave towers on the summit of
Mount Defiance is obscured by fog.

The Trail

This trail follows the boundary between Mount Hood National Forest and the Mark Hatfield Wilderness of that forest, climbing at a moderate and steady pace from beginning to end. A path at the trailhead leads left toward North Lake; you'll want to head to the right on Trail 413. Climb 0.5 mile to a junction with the Bear Lake Trail and keep right, climbing up a wide ridge with peekaboo views of Mount Hood to the south.

At 1.4 miles from the trailhead, you'll encounter a junction with the Hard Way trail (see hike #17) and the first view of the Columbia Gorge to the north and west. Keep to the right and climb to the summit of Mount Defiance, 0.2 mile farther.

I would have rated this hike higher, except for the fact that the hiker must dodge cables and microwave dishes atop Mount Defiance, which detract from the feeling of getting away from it all.

19. Starvation Creek Loop

RATING	🚶🚶🚶
DISTANCE	3.1 miles round-trip
HIKING TIME	2 hours
ELEVATION GAIN	680 feet
HIGH POINT	800 feet
DIFFICULTY LEVEL	Moderately difficult
BEST SEASON	Fall
PERMITS/CONTACT	None/Columbia River Gorge National Scenic Area, (541) 308-1700
MAPS	USGS Mount Defiance; Green Trails Hood River 430
TRAIL NOTES	Leashed dogs okay

The Hike

This short loop hike offers a short, steep climb, terrific views, and a gargling trio of waterfalls.

An interpretive sign on Gorge Trail No. 400 explains how Starvation Creek got its name.

A footbridge along Gorge Trail No. 400 crosses Cabin Creek.

Getting There

From Portland, follow Interstate 84 to Exit 54 and the rest-stop trailhead, 120 feet above sea level. To return to Portland, follow I-84 east about a mile to Viento State Park, Exit 56.

The Trail

The poorly marked trailhead is easily found in the summer, when hundreds of hikers head out on this loop. But if you're hiking this trail for the first time, the single sign pointing to "Mt. Defiance Trail Access" may be a little confusing. Begin by walking west past the paved Columbia Gorge Highway Trail along the exit road past the "Wrong Way" signs. Here, mounted facing away from the parking area, is the trailhead sign.

The path parallels the Exit 55 road for 100 yards west before dropping into the woods along I-84. In 0.3 mile, you'll arrive at a

Lancaster Falls is named after Samuel Lancaster, the designer of the Columbia River Highway.

junction with the Starvation Creek connector Trail No. 4148. Turn left and climb a series of very steep switchbacks for 0.5 mile to a junction with Starvation Ridge Trail No. 414 at **0.8** mile. If it weren't for this Achilles tendon–stretcher, this hike would be rated "moderate" and family-friendly.

Turn right onto Trail No. 414 and descend to a crossing of Cabin Creek, then climb in switchbacks around a ridge. At **1.2** miles from the trailhead, arrive at a spectacular 880-foot-high viewpoint, a good place to pause and see how far you've climbed.

The trail rounds the ridge and drops in switchbacks to a crossing of Warren Creek at **1.6** miles. You'll then climb around a broad ridge and at **1.8** miles, arrive at a junction with the Mount Defiance Trail No. 413. Stay left at this junction and follow Trail No. 413 for 0.1 mile to a view of Lancaster Falls, named for the engineer who planned the Columbia River Highway. This is a good turnaround point, at **1.9** miles, so follow Trail No. 413 back down to the junction and keep left.

The route drops into the Warren Creek canyon, where you'll cross Warren Creek. A short scramble here leads to Tunnel Falls, named

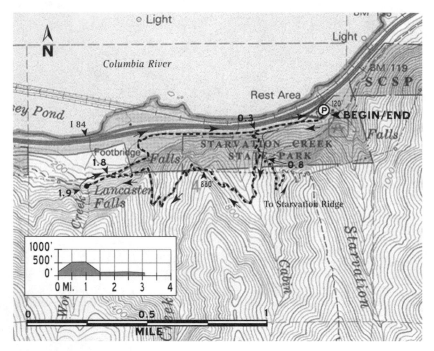

when the Columbia River Highway engineers diverted Warren Creek through a tunnel. The trail flattens and meanders through a leafy forest to cross Cabin Creek. You'll find Cabin Creek Falls hiding behind a huge boulder.

Just beyond, you'll close the loop hike at the Starvation cutoff trail. Stay left and follow the trail 0.3 mile back to the trailhead.

Going Farther

Hikers in excellent condition might enjoy the long, steep climb around the 4,960-foot summit of Mount Defiance, 11.3 miles round-trip (see hike #17). Follow the Mount Defiance Trail No. 413 past Lancaster Falls to begin the climb.

A loop hike of about 11.5 miles is also possible from the trailhead by following Starvation Creek Trail No. 414 as it climbs steeply to a junction with the Warren Lake Trail No. 417, turns right, and passes Warren Lake before descending Mount Defiance Trail No. 413 past Lancaster Falls to the trailhead.

20. Columbia River Highway– Viento State Park

RATING	🚶🚶
DISTANCE	2.2 miles round-trip
HIKING TIME	1 hour
ELEVATION GAIN	100 feet
HIGH POINT	260 feet
DIFFICULTY LEVEL	Easy
BEST SEASON	Winter
PERMITS/CONTACT	None/Columbia River Gorge National Scenic Area, (541) 308-1700
MAPS	USGS Mount Defiance; Green Trails Hood River 430
TRAIL NOTES	Leashed dogs okay; kid-friendly; bikes allowed; wheelchair accessible

The Hike

Save this walk for a rainy day when you'd like to get away from the crowds, but not necessarily from the roar of the highway. The path follows the old Columbia River Highway roadbed above Interstate 84 east and is a good warm-up trail if you'd like to hike the Starvation Creek Loop (see hike #19).

Getting There

From Portland, follow I-84 to Exit 54 and park in the rest area lot, 120 feet above sea level. To return to the westbound lanes of I-84, follow the interstate east for 1 mile to Exit 56 at Viento State Park.

The Trail

This section of the highway was closed to auto traffic in 2001, and the first 0.5 mile makes an excellent route for those who do their hiking aboard a wheelchair. The first hill from the parking area may be too steep to climb without assistance, however. The pavement gets increasingly old and at 0.8 mile, turns to crushed rock. The trail ends at the turnaround point at 1.1 miles–the paved road leading to the Viento State Park day-use area and tent campground.

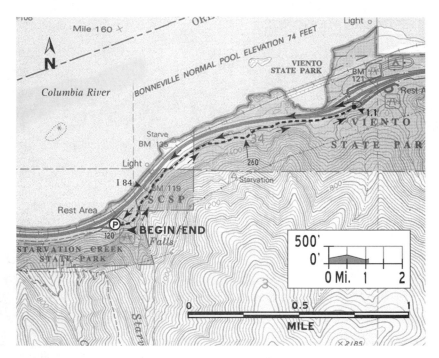

Going Farther

A way trail climbs very steeply up Viento Ridge from the Highway Trail, 0.2 mile from the trailhead. It's marked by a chain of three vertical X's carved into a vine maple tree trunk on the right side of the road.

The trail switches back up rocky open slopes and forest above Starvation Creek. It turns east along a power line before plunging steeply back to the old highway at a cable crossing sign. The second junction is marked by an arrow-shaped sign labeled "161/162." This difficult path is reserved for masochists who enjoy wading through massive patches of poison oak and steep, rocky trails that strongly resemble sheer cliffs.

21. Mitchell Point

RATING	
DISTANCE	2.4 miles round-trip
HIKING TIME	2.5 hours
ELEVATION GAIN	1,050 feet
HIGH POINT	1,178 feet
DIFFICULTY LEVEL	Difficult
BEST SEASON	Spring
PERMITS/CONTACT	None/Columbia River Gorge National Scenic Area, (541) 308-1700
MAPS	USGS Hood River; Green Trails Hood River 430
TRAIL NOTES	Leashed dogs okay

The lower cliffs of Mitchell Point are shrouded by October mist.

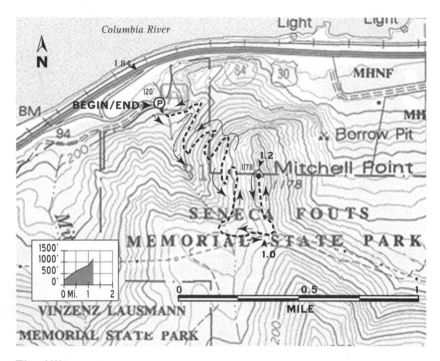

The Hike
Here's a steep, rocky climb to a fabulous view of the Columbia River Gorge and very nearly the rest of the civilized world.

Getting There
From Portland, follow Interstate 84 to the Mitchell Point Overlook, Exit 58, 120 feet above sea level. To return to the westbound lanes, follow the interstate about 4 miles east to Hood River, Exit 62.

The Trail
The trailhead is not marked. Begin by passing the Vinzenz Lausmann Memorial State Park sign on a paved path that climbs south at the south end of the Mitchell Point parking area. The pavement turns west to a plaque commemorating the Lausmann's gift to Oregon State Parks; stay left on the gravel path leading uphill and turning west to follow an old roadbed for about 300 feet before turning left and climbing into the forest.

The trail alternately passes through oak forest and rocky open slopes on a typical Columbia Gorge sharp basalt footpath. It switches back and climbs more steeply in three switchbacks

A rainbow arches over the Columbia at Mitchell Point.

underneath Mitchell Point, with views of the river, Drano Lake to the north, and Wind and Dog mountains across the river.

At **1.0** mile, you'll find a junction at a power line swath and ridge-crest saddle. Stay left and walk across the saddle to views that grow increasingly exposed and grander to the end of the trail. The final 0.1 mile of this trail is along a sharp, exposed ridge. Those who, like me, have an irrational fear of heights will likely turn back before reaching the final, breathtaking perch at **1.2** miles, 1,178 feet above the Gorge.

22. Wygant Viewpoint

RATING	🚶🚶🚶
DISTANCE	3 miles round-trip
HIKING TIME	1.5 hours
ELEVATION GAIN	280 feet
HIGH POINT	400 feet
DIFFICULTY LEVEL	Moderate
BEST SEASON	Spring, fall
PERMITS/CONTACT	None/Columbia River Gorge National Scenic Area, (541) 308-1700
MAPS	USGS Bonneville Dam, Tanner Butte; Green Trails Hood River 430
TRAIL NOTES	Leashed dogs okay; kid-friendly

The Hike

This walk follows the old Columbia River Highway before climbing to a turnaround point and grand view of the Gorge, with the option of continuing on a 6-mile loop.

The trail to Wygant Viewpoint begins on a paved trail, part of the old Columbia River Highway.

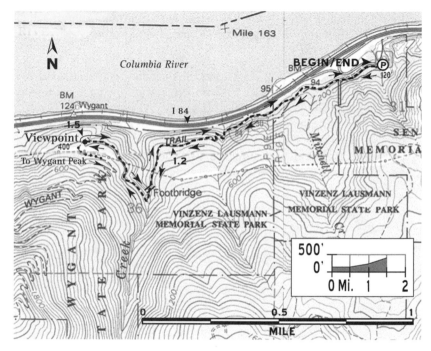

Getting There

From Portland, follow Interstate 84 to the Mitchell Point Overlook, Exit 58, 120 feet above sea level. To return to the westbound lanes, follow the interstate about 4 miles east to Hood River, Exit 62.

The Trail

The Wygant Viewpoint Trail begins at the west end of the parking area, next to the parking area entrance road. Follow the paved trail, part of the old Columbia River Highway, as it drops gently into the forest to the end of the pavement and look for a trail sign and junction to the right.

Stay right and cross Mitchell Creek before joining the old highway again. Follow the road for 0.3 mile and look left for the signed trail that leaves the road and begins a moderate climb in a couple of switchbacks to a junction with the Chetwoot Trail, 1.2 miles from the trailhead.

Pass a side trail leading to an overgrown viewpoint and descend to the Perham Creek bridge (which a sign noted was closed on a visit several years ago). Cross the creek and climb on a gentle grade for 0.3 mile to a wide viewpoint and picnic turnaround spot at 1.5 miles, 300 feet above the Columbia River.

Going Farther

A 6-mile loop can be made by taking the Chetwoot Trail as it climbs 1.0 mile along a ridge above Perham Creek, crosses the creek to a junction with the Wygant Trail at 0.5 mile. Take the Wygant Trail to the left and climb another 0.5 mile in switchbacks to a viewpoint and turnaround point. Return to the Wygant Trail junction and stay left to drop back down in 1.0 mile to cross Perham Creek and climb back to the Chetwoot Trail junction.

23. McCall Point

RATING	🚶🚶🚶🚶
DISTANCE	3 miles round-trip
HIKING TIME	2 hours
ELEVATION GAIN	1,000 feet
HIGH POINT	1,722 feet
DIFFICULTY LEVEL	Moderately difficult
BEST SEASON	Spring
PERMITS/CONTACT	None/The Nature Conservancy of Oregon, (503) 230-1221
MAPS	USGS Lyle
TRAIL NOTES	Dogs prohibited; kid-friendly

The Hike

This splendid, sunny trail leads to a superlative view through wild-flower meadows and oak forest.

Clouds gather over the Columbia at Rowena Crest, the trailhead for pathways leading to McCall Point and Rowena Plateau.

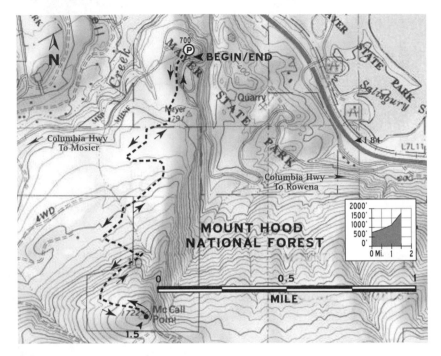

Getting There

Follow Interstate 84 from Portland to the Mosier exit, Exit 69. Turn right and follow the Historic Columbia River Highway 30 through Mosier for 6 miles to the Rowena Crest Viewpoint and trailhead, 700 feet above sea level.

The Trail

This is a Nature Conservancy Trail and pets are prohibited. The route follows a pioneer wagon route across the Rowena Plateau for 0.5 mile, spectacular with wildflowers in the early spring. Expanding views may distract the eye from the nearby color. If it's flower photos you're after, perhaps you'd best wait for that rare cloudy day.

The trail leaves the meadows to climb along an oak-covered hillside and gradually steepens in switchbacks to the summit. This picnic turnaround, at 1.5 miles from the trailhead, yields awesome views of Mounts Hood and Adams and the mighty sweep of the Columbia River.

McCall Point is named for Tom McCall, governor of Oregon from 1967 to 1975.

24. Rowena Plateau

RATING	🚶🚶🚶
DISTANCE	2.0 miles round-trip
HIKING TIME	1 hour
ELEVATION GAIN	150 feet
HIGH POINT	700 feet
DIFFICULTY LEVEL	Easy
BEST SEASON	Spring
PERMITS/CONTACT	None/The Nature Conservancy of Oregon, (503) 230-1221
MAPS	USGS Lyle
TRAIL NOTES	Dogs prohibited; kid-friendly

The Hike

Here's a short, easy hike through a meadowland table set with wildflowers of every color and description in the early spring, and with remarkable cliffside views of the Columbia River below.

Getting There

Follow Interstate 84 from Portland to the Mosier exit, Exit 69. Turn right and follow the Historic Columbia River Highway 30 through Mosier for 6 miles to the Rowena Crest Viewpoint and trailhead. The trailhead is located west across the Columbia River Highway from the parking area and begins at a sign just over a fence step, 700 feet above sea level.

The trail to Rowena Plateau leads to ponds and cliffside viewpoints above the Columbia River.

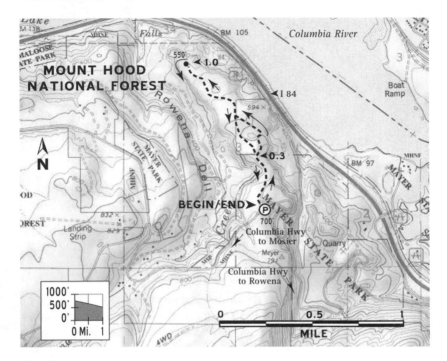

The Trail

The hike across the Governor Tom McCall Preserve on the Rowena Plateau begins at a sign that will give you some of the information about the country you'll see. At **0.3** mile, the trail drops gently to the larger of two ponds before circling it and continuing to the second.

Beyond, the trail continues in a westerly direction to the plateau edge at **1.0** mile, where you'll look south into the Rowena Dell, west down the Columbia River to Memaloose Island, and north across the river to the mouth of the Klickitat River. If, like me, you share an irrational fear of heights, you'll want to stay well back from the cliff's edges—which are rounded and offer little sure footing.

Going Farther

The short walk along the Rowena Plateau can be combined with the longer climb to McCall Point (see hike #23). Both hikes would total 5 miles, with an elevation gain of about 1,150 feet.

25. Columbia River Highway Trail

RATING	🚶🚶🚶
DISTANCE	9.2 miles round-trip
HIKING TIME	4.5 hours
ELEVATION GAIN	350 feet
HIGH POINT	580 feet
DIFFICULTY LEVEL	Moderate
BEST SEASON	Spring, fall
PERMITS/CONTACT	Northwest Forest Pass required/ Columbia River Gorge National Scenic Area, (541) 308-1700
MAPS	USGS Lyle
TRAIL NOTES	Leashed dogs okay; kid-friendly; bikes allowed; wheelchair accessible

The Hike

Walk, bike, blade, or wheel along the old Columbia River Highway on this path that has something for the whole family: views, historic tunnels, and a visitor center.

Bicycles, wheelchairs, and in-line skaters share the paved Columbia River Highway Trail through the Mosier Twin Tunnels.

Getting There

Follow Interstate 84 east from Hood River to the Mosier exit, Exit 69, turn right and follow the Historic Columbia River Highway 30 to Rock Creek Road; turn left there and follow the signs to the trailhead parking area on the left. Follow the trail signs about 150 feet back down the road to the trailhead and handicapped parking access on the west side of the road, 225 feet above sea level.

The Trail

You'll want to take this walk near the dry end of the Columbia Gorge in the early spring or later fall, when it isn't so hot. It follows a closed portion of the historic highway through two tunnels with "windows" carved in the rock that look down on the river. It's a hike for the entire family and is smooth asphalt the entire way. Except for the longer distance, it would be rated an "Easy" walk. Trailheads are located just east of Hood River and at the Mosier end. The Mosier end is likely to be less crowded and is closer to the tunnels—which is why it is recommended here.

Begin by climbing gently around a bluff to wide meadows above the Columbia River and a picnic area viewpoint. Continue as the old highway begins a long, gentle downgrade to the eastern portal of the tunnel, 0.8 mile from the trailhead. Both tunnels are about a half-mile long, and the second is more of a concrete shed that protects hikers from the basalt cliffs hunkering above. A "window"

The Columbia River Highway Trail meanders through pine woods on the dry end of the Gorge.

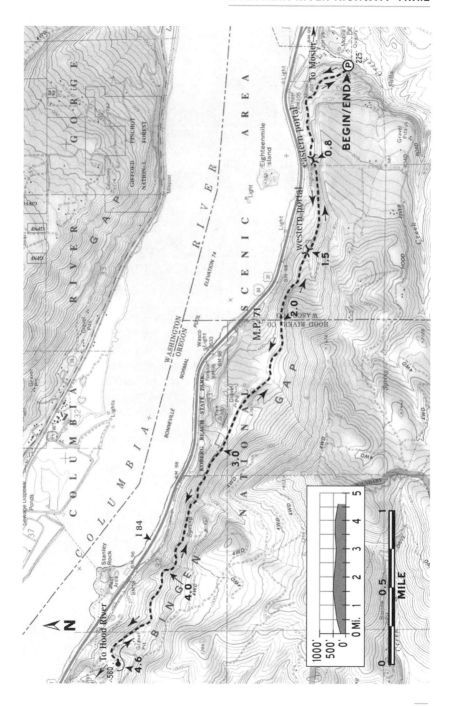

The eastern trailhead of the Columbia River Highway Trail is named after Oregon senator Mark Hatfield. It's located 0.1 mile south of the trail.

in the rock wall opens to views of the river below but now is barred for safety considerations.

The route continues to drop gently to the west end of the tunnel, then levels off through a leafy forest, where the transition between the dry sage of Mosier and the wetter climate of Hood River is most noticeable. You'll pass several historic mile markers on the highway and at the trail's end, find the Columbia Highway Visitor Center.

26. Dalles Riverfront Trail

RATING   🚶🚶🚶🚶
DISTANCE   10.4 miles round-trip
HIKING TIME   5 hours
ELEVATION GAIN   125 feet
HIGH POINT   200 feet
DIFFICULTY LEVEL   Moderate
BEST SEASON   Spring, fall
PERMITS/CONTACT   None/Columbia River Gorge National Scenic Area, (541) 308-1700
MAPS   USGS Petersburg
TRAIL NOTES   Leashed dogs okay; kid-friendly; bikes allowed; wheelchair accessible

The Hike

Portions of this all-blacktop walk along the Columbia River from the Gorge Discovery Center to The Dalles downtown waterfront park are brand-new. The trail makes a splendid hike or in-line skate in early spring, with lowland wildflowers and usual sunshine.

Getting There

Follow Interstate 84 east from Portland to The Dalles, Exit 82, about 85 miles east of Portland. Turn west and follow the signs to Discovery Center Road, 1.3 miles. Follow the road to the trailhead at the Discovery Center, 200 feet above sea level.

The Trail

A heretofore unknown secret diary of William Clark turned up in 2003 on eBay, and I was able to "buy it now" for the bargain price of $1,439.97. There is little question as to its authenticity, because the seller—P. T. Barnum IV—guaranteed my money back if I could track him down. In the entry for April 18, 1806, Clark described a strange dream he had when he "had not slept but very little for the two nights past on account of mice and vermin." The Corps of Discovery was camped at Rockfort, near the present city of The Dalles. Clark wrote: "In my dream, Capt. Lewis and Sgt. Ordway were clad in some shiny cloths that stuck to their bodies. They also wore boots with wheels attached, and rolled along a smooth black trail

The Columbia Gorge Discovery Center serves as the western trailhead
for the Dalles Riverfront Trail.

that reeked of taur. This vision I attribute to boiled roots we ate for
supper, which also filled us so full of wind that we were scarcely
able to breathe all night."

In-line skaters, joggers, bicyclists, and those who do their hiking
aboard a wheelchair may wish to start at the east end of the trail
at the boat basin in The Dalles and head west, along more level
sections of trail. The western trailhead at the Columbia Gorge Discovery Center begins with a series of switchbacks that might be too
steep or require assistance for some.

Once at river level, about 1.0 mile from the trailhead, the wide,
paved pathway meanders toward Taylor Lake and crosses a marshy
area before the pavement ends. The route continues on a section of
trail paved in 2008, then crosses a bridge 2.5 miles from the trailhead. It climbs a bank above the river in switchbacks, then begins a
long, flat route to the south and east toward The Dalles.

This final 3 miles of the trail pass two parking areas and alternate
trailheads for hikers who don't want to walk or ride the entire 10.4
round-trip miles. The trail is a splendid harbinger of the ongoing
redevelopment of The Dalles's riverfront, from an industrial waste-
land to a recreational wonderland.

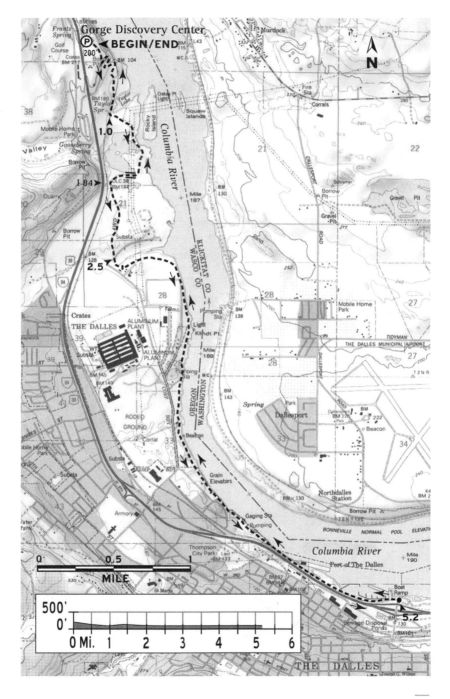

27. Deschutes River Loop

RATING	🚶🚶🚶🚶
DISTANCE	4.6 miles round-trip
HIKING TIME	3 hours
ELEVATION GAIN	640 feet
HIGH POINT	840 feet
DIFFICULTY LEVEL	Moderately difficult
BEST SEASON	Spring, fall
PERMITS/CONTACT	None/Deschutes River State Recreation Area, (800) 551-6949
MAPS	USGS Wishram, Emerson
TRAIL NOTES	Leashed dogs okay; kid-friendly

The Hike

This walk has two personalities: an easy 2-mile trek along the banks of the sparkling Deschutes River and a steeper climb into the green, wildflower-covered hills of springtime above the river.

Getting There

Follow Interstate 84 east from The Dalles about 17 miles to the Celilo exit, Exit 97. Turn right and then immediately left at the stop sign, and follow the signs to the Deschutes River State Recreation Area. The trailhead is at the southernmost parking area, across a grassy field next to the river, 200 feet above sea level.

The Deschutes River Loop hike climbs more than
400 feet above the river.

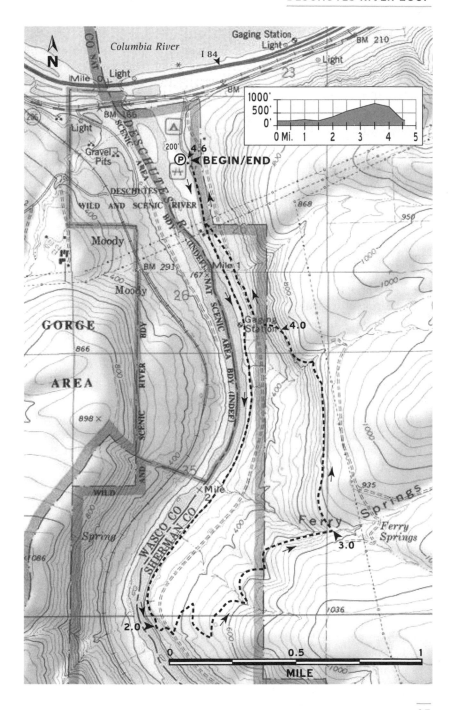

The Trail

Here, in the eastern end of the Columbia Gorge, the sun shines so often that you'll find a stay-away warning in the Official Book of Vampire Rules. Spring arrives around Valentine's Day and billions of wildflowers begin to blossom around the first week of March.

The first 2.0 miles of this trail meander along the river, where wooden benches invite you to rest in the shade and watch the Deschutes roll by. It's frequently used by anglers, who are prohibited from fishing by boat in the lower part of the river, and by birdwatchers who enjoy watching the antics of those hanging apartment-dwellers, the orioles.

At a sign directing you to the Middle and Upper Trails, at 2.0 miles, turn left and climb a steep hillside for 0.2 mile to a junction with the Middle Trail at 2.2 miles. Turn right and follow it as it climbs to join the multiuse Deschutes River Rail Trail (see hike #28). This makes a good turnaround for families with younger children, who can follow the old railroad bed back to the trailhead for a loop trip of about 4 miles. Hikers wishing to complete the longer loop might first explore the junction area, which overlooks Rattlesnake Rapids and features a small natural bridge just below the trail.

To continue, walk about 150 feet south on the rail trail to the signed Upper Trail. It begins a switchback climb through sage- and wildflower-carpeted hills, gaining about 500 feet in about a mile before turning and traversing north. You'll cross several barbed-wire fences on wooden steps and climb to the only spot of green in the fall, Ferry Springs, 3.0 miles from the trailhead. Past the springs, the trail begins a mile-long contour to the north, with spectacular views of the Deschutes River Valley below and the Horse Heaven Hills and Toppenish Ridge across the Columbia River.

At 3.8 miles from the trailhead, descend across a gully and begin dropping toward the trailhead. Cross the rail trail and close the loop at the grassy field.

Going Farther

Day hikers from Portland, Vancouver, and beyond will find the Deschutes River State Recreation Area a splendid camping spot, especially in the early spring before it gets uncomfortably hot. The campground, open year-round, makes an excellent base camp for this loop hike and the rail trail that follows. Campers can reserve sites at Deschutes by calling (800) 452-5687.

28. Deschutes River Rail Trail

RATING	🚶🚶🚶🚶
DISTANCE	9.2 miles round-trip
HIKING TIME	5 hours
ELEVATION GAIN	200 feet
HIGH POINT	400 feet
DIFFICULTY LEVEL	Moderate
BEST SEASON	Spring, fall
PERMITS/CONTACT	None/Deschutes River State Recreation Area, (800) 551-6949
MAPS	USGS Wishram, Emerson
TRAIL NOTES	Leashed dogs okay; kid-friendly; bikes allowed

The Hike

This springtime walk along an old railroad bed is a beautiful intro-
duction to the sunny, dry end of the Columbia Gorge and a great
mountain bike ride. From March through June, hay burners and
their equestrian companions are welcome.

Getting There

Follow Interstate 84 east from The Dalles about 17 miles to Celilo,
Exit 97. Turn right and immediately left at the stop sign and follow
the signs to the Deschutes River State Recreation Area. The trailhead is on the east side of the entrance road to the recreation area,
opposite the campground, at 200 feet above sea level.

The Trail

The gently graded, dirt and gravel path along the hillside above
the wild Deschutes River is suitable for pedestrians of all ages and
offers a round-trip walk (or mountain bike ride) of up to 34 miles.
Unless you enjoy power day hikes—and this would make an excellent one in early spring or late fall, when it's not uncomfortably
hot—you'll probably choose to turn around about 4.6 miles from
the trailhead.

Perhaps the steepest grade on this hike is the short climb from the
parking area to the old railroad grade, now covered with fine sand
and gravel. You'll follow the old rail trail south above the river as

The Deschutes River Rail Trail follows the river more than 17 miles upstream and is open to mountain bikes year-round and seasonally to equestrians.

it contours along sage- and wildflower-decorated hillsides. At **2.0** miles, arrive at a junction with trails descending to the river and climbing the hillside above, to the Deschutes River Loop (see hike #27). Look just below the Rattlesnake Rapids viewpoint for a small natural bridge.

Beyond, the route begins descending gently toward river flats and an old homestead, leaving a portion of the railroad grade to cross the Gordon Canyon. Below the trail, you'll see a field surrounded by a basalt rock fence built from the boulders plucked from the field. One of several pit toilets placed along the river is located here, about **3.5** miles from the trailhead. To continue, climb

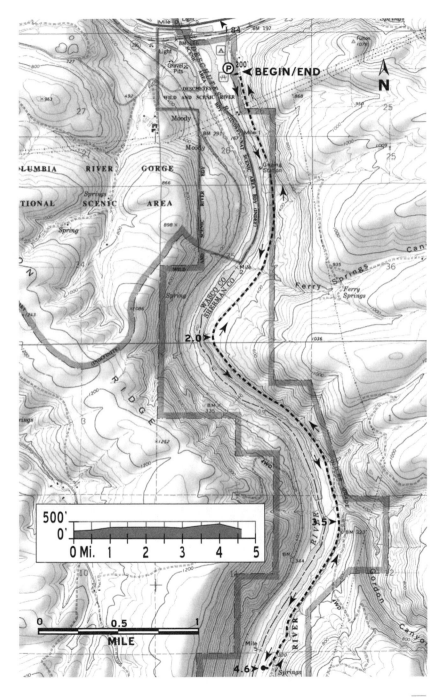

The Deschutes River Rail Trail follows the river
for about 2 miles upstream.

back up to the railroad grade and follow the trail as it crosses under basalt cliffs above the river.

A good turnaround spot, **4.6** miles from the trailhead, is at seasonal springs just below the trail. You'll look out onto the Deschutes River, more than 5 miles from its mouth at the Columbia.

Going Farther

The Deschutes River State Recreation Area features a fine trailhead campground for hikers planning a weekend outing. To reserve a site, call (800) 452-5687.

29. Klickitat Rail Trail

RATING	🚶🚶🚶🚶
DISTANCE	7.0 miles
HIKING TIME	3.5 hours
ELEVATION GAIN	120 feet
HIGH POINT	260 feet
DIFFICULTY LEVEL	Moderate
BEST SEASON	Spring, fall
PERMITS/CONTACT	None/Klickitat Trail Conservancy, www.klickitat-trail.org
MAPS	USGS Stacker Butte
TRAIL NOTES	Leashed dogs okay; kid-friendly; bikes allowed; no camping or fires

The Hike
Walk along the Klickitat River, designated a Wild and Scenic River, on one of the newest rails-to-trails in the state—or ride a mountain bike or horse up to 62 miles round-trip. You also have an opportunity for a one-way walk with a car-key trade.

Getting There
From Interstate 84 in The Dalles, take Exit 87 and cross the Columbia River on the Highway 197 bridge to Washington Highway 14. Turn left and drive 8 miles to the Highway 142 junction in Lyle. Turn right on Highway 142 and drive 3 miles to the parking area at the Fisher Hill Road bridge, marked by a sign indicating you are leaving the Columbia Gorge National Scenic Area. Cross the Fisher Hill Road bridge to find the trailhead on the right, 160 feet above sea level. Limited parking is also available across the Fisher Hill bridge, alongside the road.

Washington hikers can also follow Highway 14 east from Exit 27 in Vancouver for 70 miles to Lyle—or take I-84 from Portland to the Hood River Bridge and follow Highway 14 east 10 miles from Bingen.

The Trail
I figured I had finished hiking the Columbia Gorge trails for this book by the time I read about this walk in an issue of *Washington Trails Magazine*. Were it not for this Washington Trails Association

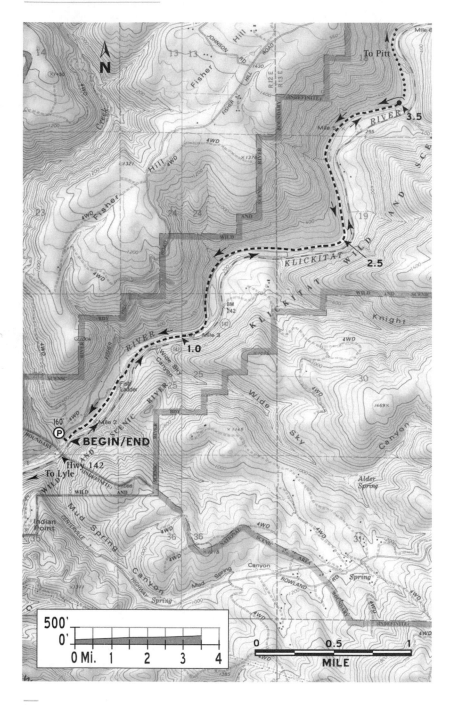

periodical, I might have missed one of the most enjoyable hikes in the eastern end of the Gorge.

Begin by crossing the Fisher Hill bridge, which passes underneath the old railroad bridge that will eventually become part of the trail once guard rails are installed. The trail follows the old Burlington Northern Railroad grade, which the volunteer Klickitat Trail Conservancy is working to turn over trail maintenance and operations to the U.S. Forest Service and Washington State Parks.

The trail passes a number of privately owned tracts and hikers are asked to stay on the old railroad right-of-way. The path is obvious, mostly covered in railroad ballast that will make hikers in soft-soled shoes regret they didn't wear heavier boots. The first mile climbs above the Klickitat River, which tumbles through a narrow gorge, passing several fishing camps. The river is popular with Native American fishers as well as sports anglers for its run of spring chinook and summer steelhead. About 1.0 mile from the trailhead, you'll cross an access road and pass the site of a Yakama Nation fish trap.

Here the narrow river gorge widens and the trail travels flats above the water. In spring, desert lupine and sunflowers color the sage, and ospreys and eagles cruise the sky above. The trail is wide and flat, which will help you avoid the poison oak that grows in profusion on either side of the path. At 1.5 miles, you'll round a curve to the north at river's edge and pass a low island in midstream.

Continue walking along the riverside as it winds north for another 2 miles to wide flats that make a good picnic spot and turnaround point, 3.5 miles from the trailhead.

Going Farther

Hikers with two cars can walk about 9 miles one-way, from the Fisher Hill bridge to the community of Pitt on Highway 142. Hikers starting south along the trail from Pitt can park on the south side of Highway 142, just after crossing the Klickitat River. Cross the highway and step over the guard rail on the north side of the bridge and walk around the south side of the trail gates. Hikers heading downriver from Pitt can arrange to meet upriver walkers at the river flats mentioned above to trade car keys.

Hikers can also connect the first 3 miles of trail from Lyle to the Fisher Hill bridge. Trailhead parking is located across Highway 14 from the realty office at the west end of town. Mountain bikers and equestrians looking for a longer ride can continue as many as 31 miles upstream, although the trail is rough in places and awaiting volunteer improvements.

30. Catherine Creek

RATING	🚶🚶🚶🚶
DISTANCE	4.6-mile loop
HIKING TIME	2.5 hours
ELEVATION GAIN	1,120 feet
HIGH POINT	1,320 feet
DIFFICULTY LEVEL	Moderate
BEST SEASON	Spring
PERMITS/CONTACT	None/Columbia River Gorge National Scenic Area, (541) 308-1700
MAPS	USGS Lyle, White Salmon
TRAIL NOTES	Leashed dogs okay

The Hike

The evolving trails of Catherine Creek are among the best early-spring wildflower hikes in the Columbia Gorge, with splendid scenery and geologic features making the hike worthwhile year-round.

Getting There

From Portland, follow Interstate 84 to Hood River, Exit 64, and cross the Columbia River toll bridge (75 cents per car in 2010) to Highway 14. Turn right and follow Highway 14 for 5.8 miles to

The Columbia River Gorge stretches east from the Catherine Creek trails.

The lower portion of trails at Catherine Creek is paved and can be navigated in a wheelchair with assistance.

Old Highway 8 at Rowland Lake. Turn left on Old Highway 8 and drive 1.5 miles to the trailhead on the left side of the road, 280 feet above sea level.

The Trail

The loop hike that follows Catherine Creek into wide meadows and grassland would make a fine family-friendly walk, assuming the youngsters can identify and avoid the poison oak that grows here and can recognize the occasional rattlesnake they might encounter. Relax, though—you're more likely to be joined by hundreds of wildflower enthusiasts in the spring than by snakes or three-leaved plants that make you itch.

In the summer of 2010, volunteers and Forest Service workers were improving the trails around Catherine Creek. Begin by following a rocky road identified by a trailhead post No. 015 that climbs to the left from the gated trailhead. The way eventually

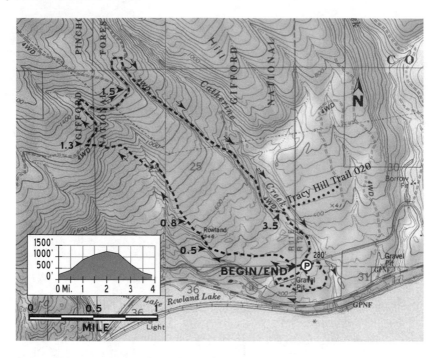

turns to single-track and climbs and dips for 0.5 mile through stands of oak and pine trees, painted in the spring by hundreds of varieties of wildflowers.

At the top of Rowland Ridge, you'll find an unmarked trail junction and turn right to climb along the top of basalt cliffs decorated with poison oak. Scramble another 0.3 mile to a second trail junction and keep right to climb across basalt plateaus and prairies below ever-present Gorge power lines. Drop into and climb steeply out of a gully to join an abandoned jeep track, 1.3 miles from the trailhead. Follow the track to the right and cross under the power lines for 0.25 mile to another trail junction, where you'll keep right on the track. The route turns downhill through a stand of fir and oak trees, closer to Catherine Creek.

The trail drops to the creek, where it joins with Tracy Hill Trail 020 3.5 miles from the trailhead, then follows the creek before turning back to the trailhead. Your hike doesn't end here, however, because you can cross the highway to the paved nature trails that loop down to a waterfall as Catherine Creek drops into the Gorge, and climbs to generous views of the Columbia River.

Going Farther

The Tracy Hill Trail 020 crosses Catherine Creek on a plank bridge, passes an old homestead, and joins a side trail that leads to a natural basalt arch. The main trail climbs for 2.3 miles through open fields to a pond and grasslands that seem to stretch beyond the horizon.

31. Dog Mountain Trail No. 147

RATING	🥾🥾🥾🥾
DISTANCE	6.0 miles round-trip
HIKING TIME	3.5 hours
ELEVATION GAIN	2,800 feet
HIGH POINT	2,948 feet
DIFFICULTY LEVEL	Difficult
BEST SEASON	Spring, fall
PERMITS/CONTACT	Northwest Forest Pass required/Wind River Ranger District, (509) 427-5171
MAPS	USGS Mount Defiance; Green Trails Hood River 430
TRAIL NOTES	Leashed dogs okay

The Hike

Join the throngs who annually make the tough climb to meadows near the summit of Dog Mountain to admire spectacular wildflower displays and get one of the best views of the Columbia River Gorge from an old Forest Service lookout site.

Getting There

From Interstate 84 take Cascade Locks, Exit 44, about 41 miles east of Portland, and cross the Bridge of the Gods ($1 in 2011) to Washington Highway 14. Turn right and drive 12 miles to the wide Dog

Dog Mountain Trail No. 147 is the most direct route to the summit.

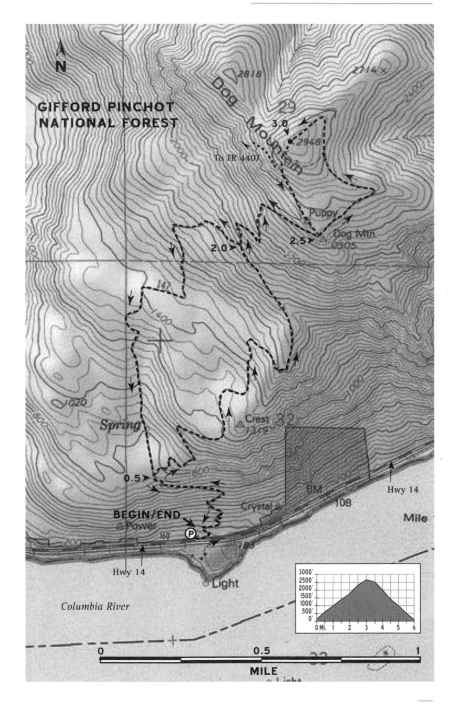

N

GIFFORD PINCHOT
NATIONAL FOREST

Dog Mountain

2818

2714 X

29

3.0

2948

To TR 4407

Puppy

2.5

Dog Mtn
2505

2.0

147

1400

Crest
1319

32

1020

Spring

BM

Hwy 14

0.5

800

108

Mile

BEGIN/END
Power

160'

P

Crystal

Hwy 14

Light

Columbia River

3000'								
2500'								
2000'								
1500'								
1000'								
500'								
0'								
0 Mi.	1	2	3	4	5	6		

0   0.5   1
MILE

32

Light

Mountain parking area and trailhead on the left, 160 feet above sea level. Washington residents who don't mind a two-lane highway can follow scenic Highway 14 for 46 miles east from Exit 27 off Interstate 205 in Vancouver.

The Trail

Meriwether Lewis wrote of this region on June 12, 1806: "The quamish [camas] is now in blume . . . and there always in open grounds and glades."

Expect company on this trail almost any time of the year, although you may find weekdays in late fall when you'll have the hike pretty much to yourself. The hike is especially popular in spring, when more than a hundred cars overflow the parking area and all paths to the summit teem with two-hooved animals.

Still, this is one of the hikes that shouldn't be missed. Wildflowers are spectacular in spring, provided you can tear your eyes away from the views west down the Columbia Gorge or across the river to Mount Hood. Hikers who are ogling views or flowers should also take care where they put their feet: Poison oak is common along the trail, and rattlesnakes sun themselves on the south-facing slopes.

The shorter and steeper of two loop hikes begins at the eastern end of the parking area and wastes little time getting into the spirit of the climb. You'll switchback up a steep path for 700 vertical feet to a junction with the Old Trail No. 147 and the Scenic Trail, at 0.5 mile from the trailhead. For the loop trip, turn right on the newer— some say more gentle—Scenic Trail.

At **2.0** miles from the trailhead, you'll rejoin the Old Trail No. 147 and climb 0.5 mile to a junction that loops around and over the Dog Mountain summit. Stay right and climb to a steep ridge to the east and turn back to the top of the peak, **3.0** miles from the trailhead.

To return, follow the trail over the summit to a junction with Trail No. 4407 and stay right to descend to the junction with Old Trail No. 147, closing the summit loop. Turn right and descend 0.5 mile to the lower loop, following Old Trail No. 147 to the right, which drops steeply to close the lower loop **0.5** mile from the trailhead. Keep right to descend to the trailhead—unless you're a superhiker and want to do the whole thing again.

32. Dog Mountain Trail No. 4407

RATING	🚶🚶🚶
DISTANCE	7.1 miles round-trip
HIKING TIME	4 hours
ELEVATION GAIN	2,800 feet
HIGH POINT	2,948 feet
DIFFICULTY LEVEL	Difficult
BEST SEASON	Spring, fall
PERMITS/CONTACT	Northwest Forest Pass required/Wind River Ranger District, (509) 427-5171
MAPS	USGS Mount Defiance; Green Trails Hood River 430
TRAIL NOTES	Leashed dogs okay

The Hike

This longer climb to the summit of Dog Mountain offers the same spectacular views and wildflower displays with a more gentle descent back to the trailhead. The 1.5-mile traverse under the summit of Dog Mountain yields awesome views of the Columbia Gorge and just about everything east of Hawaii—or nearly so.

Getting There

From Interstate 84 take Cascade Locks, Exit 44, about 41 miles east of Portland, and cross the Bridge of the Gods ($1 in 2011) to Washington Highway 14. Turn right and drive 12 miles to the wide Dog Mountain parking area and trailhead on the left, 160 feet above sea level. Washington residents who don't mind a two-lane highway can follow scenic Highway 14 for 46 miles east from Exit 27 off Interstate 205 in Vancouver.

The Trail

Begin with the steep, 700-foot climb for **0.5** mile up Dog Mountain Trail No. 147 to the junction with the Old Trail No. 147 and the Scenic Trail. Stay left here and climb the Old Trail No. 147, which is a steeper but more direct path to the summit. Rejoin the Scenic Trail **1.9** miles from the trailhead, climb another 0.5 mile to a loop trail across the summit, turn left at **2.4** miles and climb steeply to the summit at **3.0** miles, passing the Augspurger connector to the right.

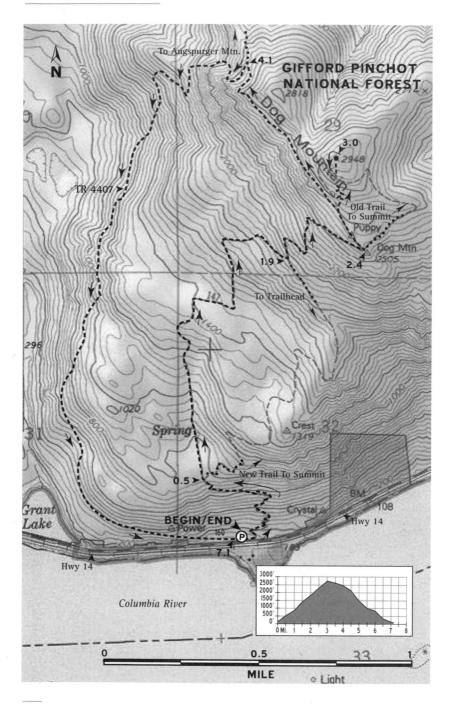

Hikers descend Dog Mountain Trail No. 4407.

Once you've exhausted your film, filled your digital camera, and rested up, descend to the Augspurger connector, turn right, and traverse the open slopes of Dog Mountain to a junction with Augspurger Trail No. 4407, 4.1 miles from the trailhead. Turn left and begin a steady, 3.0-mile descent to the parking area, 200 feet west of the Dog Mountain trailhead.

33. Pacific Crest Trail 2000, Gillette Lake

RATING	🥾🥾
DISTANCE	4.6 miles round-trip
HIKING TIME	2.5 hours
ELEVATION GAIN	420 feet
HIGH POINT	400 feet
DIFFICULTY LEVEL	Moderate
BEST SEASON	Spring, fall
PERMITS/CONTACT	Northwest Forest Pass required/ Gifford Pinchot National Forest, (360) 696-7500
MAPS	USGS Bonneville Dam; Green Trails Bonneville Dam 429
TRAIL NOTES	Leashed dogs okay; kid-friendly

The Hike

Here's a taste of the first few Washington miles of the granddaddy of all wilderness pathways, Pacific Crest Trail (PCT) 2000. You'll distance yourself from most of civilization to a pleasant lake along the trail.

Getting There

From Interstate 84 take Cascade Locks, Exit 44, about 41 miles east of Portland, and cross the Bridge of the Gods ($1 in 2011) to Washington Highway 14. Turn left and drive 2 miles to the parking area just across Highway 14 from the Bonneville Dam Visitor Center. Turn right into the parking lot and trailhead, 80 feet above sea level.

Washington residents who don't mind a two-lane highway can follow scenic Highway 14 for about 34 miles east from Exit 27 off Interstate 205 in Vancouver. Turn left into the parking area directly across from the Bonneville Dam Visitor Center.

The Trail

Day hikers will find this short climb to the PCT 2000 more accommodating than the official Washington trailhead for the PCT, located about 1.5 miles to the east. From the parking area, follow Trail No. 27 as it climbs through conifer forest to a bench

A shady rest stop along the Pacific Crest Trail 2000 to Gillette Lake.

above the Columbia River. At **0.3** mile, you'll find a cleared viewpoint with a glance up the Columbia River and Highway 14 below.

The trail continues along the bench, climbing gently, rounding a wide gully, and finally descending to a junction with the PCT at **0.7** mile. Turn left here and follow the trail as it drops gently, then climbs in 0.3 mile to a wide clear-cut area, which can be hot and dry on summer days.

The trail drops through the clear-cut, then climbs along the edge of the forest for 0.5 mile. You'll drop to a shaded saddle before climbing over a 400-foot hill, then descend to cross a road underneath power lines to Gillette Lake, the turnaround point at **2.3** miles.

Going Farther

Wilderness walkers looking for more exercise can continue along the PCT for another 0.8 mile to a crossing of Greenleaf Creek, then climb to an 800-foot-high hill overlooking the Columbia Gorge, 4 miles from the trailhead. Of course, if you want a real day hike, you

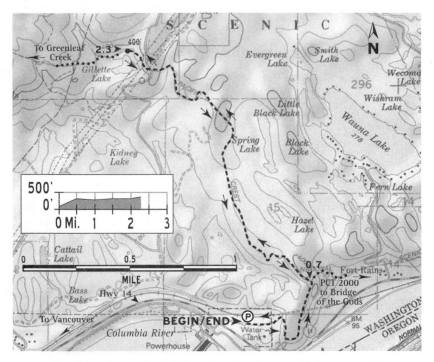

can head north on the PCT to Canada—but you'll have to pick up
your pace if you plan to make it in a day.

34. The Dam Loop

RATING	 🚶
DISTANCE	1.2 miles round-trip
HIKING TIME	45 minutes
ELEVATION GAIN	20 feet
HIGH POINT	40 feet
DIFFICULTY LEVEL	Easy
BEST SEASON	Spring
PERMITS/CONTACT	None/Columbia Gorge Interpretive Center, (800) 991-2338
MAPS	USGS Bonneville Dam; Green Trails Bonneville Dam 429
TRAIL NOTES	Leashed dogs okay; kid-friendly

The Hike

Short. Flat. Big Bonneville Dam view. Historic. Here's a great warm-up for nearby hikes to Gillette Lake or Hamilton Mountain.

Getting There

From Interstate 84 take Cascade Locks, Exit 44, about 41 miles east of Portland, and cross the Bridge of the Gods ($1 in 2011) to Washington Highway 14. Turn left and drive 3.2 miles to the Hamilton Island fishing access road and turn left. Follow the road to the right, then left to the Fort Cascades parking area, 40 feet above sea level.

The view of the Bonneville Dam from the Dam Loop Trail.

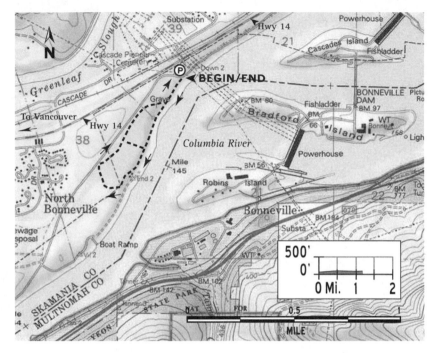

Washington residents who don't mind a two-lane highway can follow scenic Highway 14 for 32 miles east from Exit 27 off Interstate 205 in Vancouver. Turn right on the Hamilton Island fishing access road to the Fort Cascades parking area.

The Trail

This easy, pleasant walk through the woods is a good way to start the morning before heading to something a bit more challenging. Although the trail circles a National Historic site, don't expect to see much more than a collection of rusting machinery and interpretive signs pointing into the brush where a fort, a settler's grave, stables, and a blacksmith shop once existed.

Pick up a Fort Cascades Trail Guide at a kiosk at the trailhead and walk along the banks of the Columbia River for 0.1 mile to the junction with the return trail. Stay left at the junction 0.3 mile from the trailhead and continue past signs pointing into the brush at the old Fort Cascades townsite. Just past a sign pointing into the brush where pioneer Thomas McNatt's hotel stood, you'll turn back toward the trailhead, passing several more signs pointing into the brush where other buildings once existed.

35. Wind Mountain

RATING	𝍫 𝍫 𝍫
DISTANCE	2.6 miles
HIKING TIME	1.5 hours
ELEVATION GAIN	1,100 feet
HIGH POINT	1,903 feet
DIFFICULTY LEVEL	Moderately difficult
BEST SEASON	Spring, summer
PERMITS/CONTACT	None/Columbia River Gorge National Scenic Area, (541) 308-1700
MAPS	USGS Mount Defiance; Green Trails Bonneville Dam 429
TRAIL NOTES	Leashed dogs okay; kid-friendly

The Hike

This climb to an ancient Native American religious and cultural site offers the same splendid views of the Columbia Gorge as nearby Dog Mountain, without the strenuous climb. Perhaps because the trail isn't shown on any maps, the path is less crowded than many viewpoint hikes.

Getting There

From Interstate 84 take Cascade Locks, Exit 44, about 41 miles east of Portland, and cross the Bridge of the Gods ($1 in 2011) to Washington Highway 14. Turn right and drive 9 miles to the Wind Mountain Road, about 1 mile east of the Wind River Bridge. Turn left and follow Wind Mountain Road, which becomes Home Valley Road, for 1.4 miles to Girl Scout Camp Road, turn right and drive 0.3 mile to the end of the pavement and parking area. The unsigned trailhead, 850 feet above sea level, is located 0.1 mile east, down the gravel road on the right.

Washington residents who don't mind a two-lane highway can follow scenic Highway 14 for 43 miles east from Exit 27 off Interstate 205 in Vancouver, then follow the directions above.

The Trail

Begin by climbing into an evergreen forest along a steep hillside, rounding the eastern slope of the cone of Wind Mountain. The peak got its shape as the core of an ancient volcano.

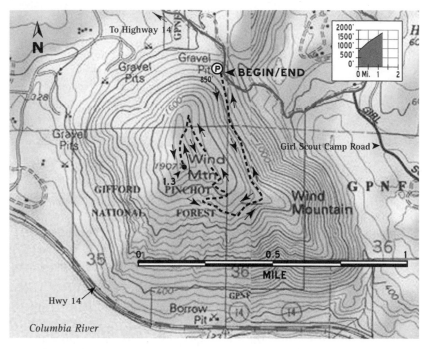

The trail climbs steadily along the eastern side of the mountain, which is more often than not sheltered from the prevailing westerly afternoon winds of the Columbia Gorge. After **0.5** mile, you'll pass a steep way trail that leads to a rock overlook. Keep right on the main trail and begin climbing a ridge in switchbacks to the north. The final climb to the summit rounds the north face and approaches from the south.

An interpretive sign at the top, **1.3** miles from the trailhead, explains the likely significance of the peak to Native Americans, and hikers are asked to take care to stay on the trail so as not to disturb the archeological site. You'll get peekaboo views through trees of Mounts St. Helens, Adams, and Hood, as well as the west end of the Columbia Gorge.

36. Sams-Walker Picnic Area

RATING	🚶
DISTANCE	1.1 miles round-trip
HIKING TIME	30 minutes
ELEVATION GAIN	20 feet
HIGH POINT	50 feet
DIFFICULTY LEVEL	Easy
BEST SEASON	Spring; open year-round
PERMITS/CONTACT	None/Columbia River Gorge National Scenic Area, (541) 308-1700
MAPS	USGS Beacon Rock; Green Trails Bridal Veil 428
TRAIL NOTES	Leashed dogs okay; kid-friendly

The Hike

If you're looking for a pleasant picnic spot on a riverside loop trail, try the Sams-Walker area. It's minutes from the trails of Beacon Rock and a quiet alternative to the crowds you'll likely find there.

Sams-Walker Picnic Area trail circles a riverside orchard.

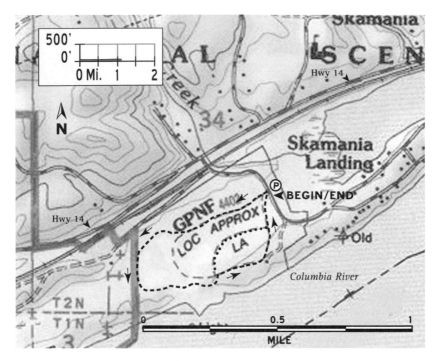

Getting There

From Interstate 84 take Cascade Locks, Exit 44, about 41 miles east of Portland, and cross the Bridge of the Gods ($1 in 2011) to Washington Highway 14. Turn left and drive 7.9 miles to Skamania. Turn left just across from the Skamania Store and follow it about 0.1 mile to the parking area on the right, 40 feet above sea level.

Washington residents who don't mind a two-lane highway can follow scenic Highway 14 for 26 miles east from Exit 27 off Interstate 205 in Vancouver, turn right at the Skamania Store and follow the road 0.1 mile to the parking area.

The Trail

This level loop walk leads around the grassy river flats, with views across the river to the cliffs of Saint Peters Dome. It's a restful spot for hikers who are looking to cool their feet from a climb up Hamilton Mountain.

37. St. Cloud Picnic Loops

RATING	 (walking figure icon)
DISTANCE	0.5 mile round-trip
HIKING TIME	30 minutes
ELEVATION GAIN	20 feet
HIGH POINT	50 feet
DIFFICULTY LEVEL	Easy
BEST SEASON	Spring; open year-round
PERMITS/CONTACT	None/Columbia River Gorge National Scenic Area, (541) 308-1700
MAPS	USGS Beacon Rock; Green Trails Bridal Veil 428
TRAIL NOTES	Leashed dogs okay; kid-friendly

The Hike

Here's a quiet stroll through an old orchard that likely glows with springtime blossoms—but makes a good picnic spot most any time of year.

The short trails at St. Cloud Picnic Area cross a green meadow to the river.

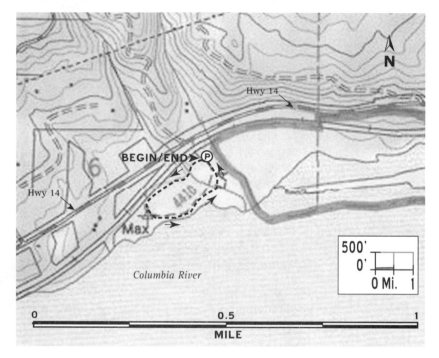

Getting There

From Interstate 84 take Cascade Locks, Exit 44, about 41 miles east of Portland, and cross the Bridge of the Gods ($1 in 2011) to Washington Highway 14. Turn left and drive a 10.8-mile access road leading to the St. Cloud Picnic Area on the left. Cross the railroad tracks to the trailhead parking area, 40 feet above sea level.

Washington residents who don't mind a two-lane highway can follow scenic Highway 14 for 23.1 miles east from Exit 27 off Interstate 205 in Vancouver and turn right at the St. Cloud Picnic Area access road.

The Trail

Here's another walk through an old riverside orchard with views of the Columbia River, Skamania Island, the forested canyon of Multnomah Falls, and the summit of Larch Mountain across the river. This trail is a good place to wind up the day from longer hikes at Beacon Rock or Gillette Lake.

38. Hardy and Rodney Falls

RATING	🚶🚶🚶
DISTANCE	2.6 miles round-trip
HIKING TIME	1.5 hours
ELEVATION GAIN	640 feet
HIGH POINT	1,000 feet
DIFFICULTY LEVEL	Moderate
BEST SEASON	Spring, fall
PERMITS/CONTACT	None/Beacon Rock State Park, (509) 427-8265
MAPS	USGS Beacon Rock; Green Trails Bridal Veil 428
TRAIL NOTES	Leashed dogs okay; kid-friendly

The Hike

Take this pleasant walk through forest in the spring, when the falls are likely to be filled with the snows and rains of winter.

Getting There

From Interstate 84 take Cascade Locks, Exit 44, about 41 miles east of Portland, and cross the Bridge of the Gods ($1 in 2011) to Washington Highway 14. Turn left and drive 6.5 miles to Beacon Rock State Park. Turn right at the picnic area and campground road, and follow it 0.3 mile to the picnic area and trailhead, 360 feet above sea level.

Washington residents who don't mind a two-lane highway can follow scenic Highway 14 for 27.5 miles east from Exit 27 off Interstate 205 in Vancouver, then turn left on the campground road and follow it to the picnic area and trailhead.

The Trail

The entire family will enjoy this climb through a mainly forested hillside along an excellent trail to two waterfalls. Begin by climbing past Little Beacon Rock, on the left, to the sunny patch created by power lines from nearby Bonneville Dam.

You'll arrive at a trail junction just above the power lines, 0.5 mile from the trailhead. Stay right here and begin climbing north around a round ridge where you can hear the sound of

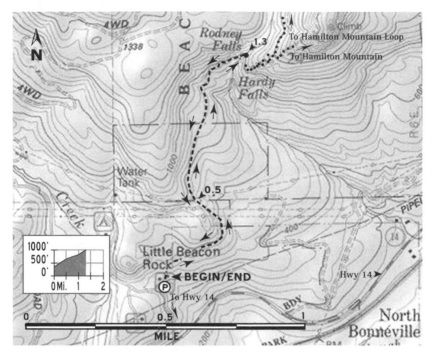

tumbling Hardy Creek off your right shoulder. The rush of the water gets louder as you approach the falls and cross a tumbling tributary creek.

At 1.2 miles, you'll see a spur trail that leads right to a view of Hardy Falls, the lower waterfall. After you're back on the main trail, continue climbing to a spur trail to the left to the Pool of Winds between Hardy and Rodney Falls. From here, the main trail climbs, then drops to a bridge across Hardy Creek, the turnaround point at 1.3 miles. The trail continues climbing to Hamilton Mountain (see hike #39).

39. Hamilton Mountain

RATING	🚶🚶🚶🚶🚶
DISTANCE	6.4 miles round-trip
HIKING TIME	4 hours
ELEVATION GAIN	2,080 feet
HIGH POINT	2,438 feet
DIFFICULTY LEVEL	Difficult
BEST SEASON	Summer, fall
PERMITS/CONTACT	None/Beacon Rock State Park, (509) 427-8265
MAPS	USGS Beacon Rock; Green Trails Bridal Veil 428
TRAIL NOTES	Leashed dogs okay

The Hike

Here's a walk that has just about everything the best Columbia Gorge trails have to offer: splendid vistas, waterfalls, alpine-style meadows filled with wildflowers, and a tough workout.

Getting There

From I-84 take Cascade Locks, Exit 44, about 41 miles east of Portland, and cross the Bridge of the Gods ($1 in 2011) to Washington Highway 14. Turn left and drive 6.5 miles to Beacon Rock State Park. Turn right at the picnic area and campground road and follow it 0.3 mile to the picnic area and trailhead, 360 feet above sea level.

Equestrians can use a separate trailhead to reach Hamilton Mountain.

Washington residents who don't mind a two-lane highway can follow scenic Highway 14 for 27.5 miles east from Exit 27 off Interstate 205 in Vancouver, then turn left on the campground road and follow it to the picnic area and trailhead.

The Trail

Begin by following the trail past Hardy and Rodney Falls (see hike #38), to the bridge crossing Hardy Creek. The serious climbing begins just across the bridge with a long traverse to the southeast, switching back and at 1.6 miles from the trailhead, arriving at a junction with a trail that closes a loop over the summit of Hamilton Mountain.

Stay right, here, and begin climbing about two-dozen switchbacks up the main south ridge of Hamilton Mountain. The views become expansive and several spur trails lead to views up and down the Columbia Gorge. The most spectacular viewpoint yields a rock perch 2.3 miles from the trailhead. You'll look down on Beacon Rock and across the Columbia to Tanner Butte. This is a good picnic spot when winds aren't strong, and families with younger children may want to turn around here.

Beyond, the trail begins to climb again, traversing the hillside with peekaboo views through sparse forest of the Hardy Creek canyon and Hamilton Mountain, directly ahead. You'll climb to the long, exposed summit ridge on a series of steep switchbacks on the open crest, reaching a trail junction at the top where a way trail leads to a viewpoint to the right. To the left, the trail heads along the summit ridge and the longer loop hike. The turnaround point is 3.2 miles from the trailhead.

The view from Hamilton Mountain is at least as good as that from Dog Mountain but doesn't draw the same large crowds. Wildflowers on the upper slopes in the early summer are splendid; the forest on the lower trail yields fine displays of springtime wildflowers.

Going Farther

To make a loop trip of the climb to Hamilton Mountain, turn left at the summit trail junction and walk the summit ridge north to a junction with a state park access road. Follow the road downhill as it traverses, then switches back twice along the hillside above Hardy Creek. Look for a trail junction as the road crosses the creek. The trail follows the hillside on the east side of the creek to the junction above Rodney Falls, 2.6 miles from the summit. Total distance on the loop hike is 7.6 miles.

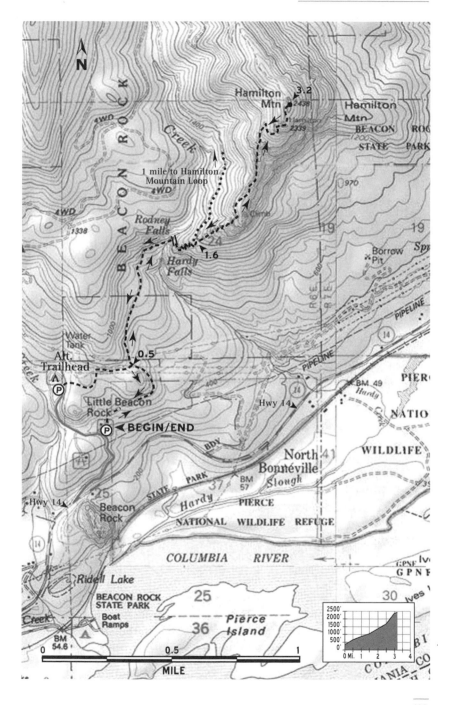

N

Hamilton
Mtn
3.2
2438

Hamilton
Mtn
2339

BEACON
STATE

ROC
PARK

970

1 mile to Hamilton
Mountain Loop
4WD

Rodney
Falls

Hardy
Falls

1.6

Borrow
Pit

Spr

Water
Tank

0.5

Alt.
Trailhead

Little Beacon
Rock

BEGIN/END

Hwy 14

BM 49
Hardy

PIER

NATIO

WILDLIFE

North
Bonneville
Slough

BM
57

PIERCE

Hwy 14

Beacon
Rock

Hardy

NATIONAL WILDLIFE REFUGE

COLUMBIA   RIVER

Ridell Lake

25

30

BEACON ROCK
STATE PARK

Boat
Ramps

36

Pierce
Island

BM
54.6

0   0.5   1

MILE

40. Beacon Rock

RATING	🚶🚶🚶🚶
DISTANCE	2.0 miles round-trip
HIKING TIME	1 hour
ELEVATION GAIN	600 feet
HIGH POINT	848 feet
DIFFICULTY LEVEL	Moderate
BEST SEASON	Summer, spring
PERMITS/CONTACT	None/Beacon Rock State Park, (509) 427-8265
MAPS	USGS Beacon Rock; Green Trails Bridal Veil 428
TRAIL NOTES	Leashed dogs okay; kid-friendly

The Hike

Although short, the climb to the top of Beacon Rock is high on the must-do list of trails in the Columbia Gorge, if for no other reason than to admire the engineering that went into the path blasted from basalt. This makes a good combination hike with those to Rodney Falls or Hamilton Mountain.

Getting There

From Interstate 84 take Cascade Locks, Exit 44, about 41 miles east of Portland, and cross the Bridge of the Gods ($1 in 2011) to Washington Highway 14. Turn left and drive 6.5 miles to Beacon Rock State Park. The Beacon Rock trailhead is the wide parking area on the left, 250 feet above sea level.

Washington residents who don't mind a two-lane highway can follow scenic Highway 14 for 27.5 miles east from Exit 27 off Interstate 205 in Vancouver, then park in the wide parking area to the right at Beacon Rock State Park.

The Trail

William Clark wrote about this region on Halloween 1805: "A remarkable high detached rock stands in a bottom on the starboard side near the lower point of this island on the starboard side about 800 feet high and 400 paces around. We call it the Beacon Rock."

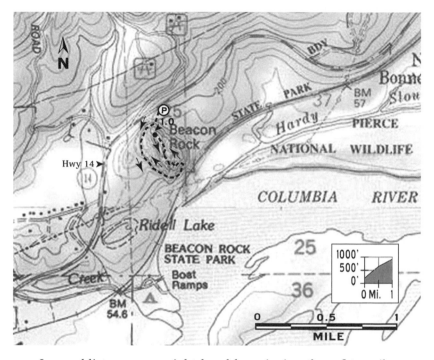

I wore blisters on my right hand by gripping the safety rail on the way to the summit of Beacon Rock, a likelihood if you, like me, have an irrational fear of heights. I balanced things out on the return by raising blisters on my left hand. Like any true acrophobe, I spent even more time worrying about other fools like my wife, B. B. Hardbody, who walked blithely along admiring the view. She totally ignored the fact that if that rail weren't there, or the wide sidewalk of the trail didn't exist, or she were blind or drunk, she would surely plunge to her death.

The trail is straightforward and climbs the cliffs of Beacon Rock in switchbacks, sometimes crossing above itself on concrete ramps. It scales the west, south, and east sides of the monolith. The trail was begun in 1916 to the airy summit, **1.0** mile from the trailhead, with views up and down the Columbia Gorge. I expected vistas of Mount Hood and Mount Adams—but the hills on either side of the Gorge block the view.

MOUNT HOOD NORTH

Hikes on the north side of Mount Hood often are in a rain shadow.

MOUNT HOOD NORTH

The country along the north and east side of Mount Hood serves up a wide variety of trails, from oak-covered hillsides to moss-draped forests. You'll find rhododendron glades in the early summer and berry patches in the fall that can turn an infinite number of tongues purple.

Though not as likely to be as warm as the southern slopes of Mount Adams, the hikes on the north side of Mount Hood may actually be less rain prone. The mountain forms a barrier to the major storms headed inland from the southwest, and there's a bit of a rain shadow to the northeast of the mountain. When it's a soggy day in the Gorge, you might find some of the lowland trails along the Highway 35 corridor to be pleasantly dry.

Until recently, my hiking on Mount Hood was confined to the area around Timberline, on the opposite side of the volcano. So Cloud Cap and the Timberline Trail on the north side of the mountain were new. If you try a few of the trails here, I'll bet you'll be as eager as I am to return.

41. Tilly Jane Loop

RATING	
DISTANCE	2.6 miles round-trip
HIKING TIME	2 hours
ELEVATION GAIN	900 feet
HIGH POINT	6,600 feet
DIFFICULTY LEVEL	Moderately difficult
BEST SEASON	Fall, summer
PERMITS/CONTACT	Northwest Forest Pass required/Hood River Ranger District, Mount Hood National Forest, (541) 352-6002
MAPS	USGS Mount Hood North; Green Trails Mount Hood 462
TRAIL NOTES	Leashed dogs okay; kid-friendly

The north face of Mount Hood dominates the view on the Tilly Jane Loop.

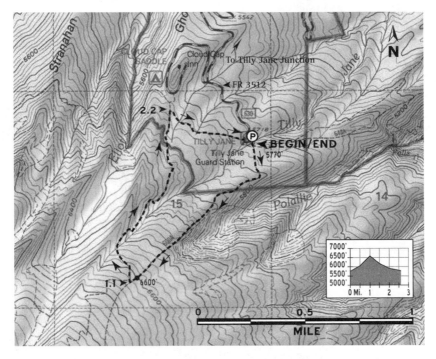

The Hike

This alpine hike is mostly above timberline and offers expansive views of the Columbia Basin, the Hood River Valley, Mount Hood, and other snow giants to the north, including Mount Adams. Save it for a sunny fall stroll.

Getting There

Follow Interstate 84 east to Hood River and take Exit 64 to the four-way stop sign. Follow Highway 35 south for about 22 miles to Forest Road 3510, turn left and follow it about 2.5 miles to the Cooper Spur Inn and FR 3512, the Cooper Spur/Tilly Jane Road. Turn left on FR 3512 and follow it past a Sno-Park area and 9.5 bumpy miles to the Cloud Cap–Tilly Jane Campground Junction. Turn left and drive 0.5 mile to the Tilly Jane Campground. The trailhead is located at the southern end of the campground, past the ranger station, at 5,770 feet above sea level.

The Trail

It may be difficult to believe that you are standing fewer than 25 miles, as the raven swoops, from the Columbia River Gorge. You've climbed more than a mile above sea level from the river and stand near timberline in the historic Tilly Jane Campground.

Begin by dropping down and crossing Tilly Jane Creek, a good source of water for hikers with filter bottles or pumps, then climb past a shelter to a junction with Trail No. 643A. Stay right on Trail No. 600A at the junction and begin a moderately steep climb along the edge of a canyon gouged by Polallie Creek.

The trail continues to climb steeply, barely hinting at switchbacks, along the canyon edge. About 0.5 mile from the trailhead, you'll climb above timberline and look uphill to the snowfield or rocky headwaters of Polallie Creek and the sharp spine of Cooper Spur. From here, the trail climbs another 0.6 mile to a junction with the Timberline Trail No. 600, 1.1 miles from the trailhead. This is an excellent spot to catch your breath, picnic, and take in the splendid view.

To continue, turn right and follow Trail No. 600 as it traverses, then descends to Cooper Spur Ridge. The trail alternates between volcanic sand and rock as it drops into an alpine evergreen forest. About 100 feet above Cloud Cap Campground, you'll reach a junction with Trail No. 600A, 2.2 miles from your starting point. Turn right and follow Trail No. 600A for 0.4 mile back to the trailhead.

42. Cooper Spur

RATING	🚶🚶🚶🚶🚶
DISTANCE	5.8 miles round-trip
HIKING TIME	3.5 hours
ELEVATION GAIN	2,640 feet
HIGH POINT	8,400 feet
DIFFICULTY LEVEL	Difficult
BEST SEASON	Fall, summer
PERMITS/CONTACT	Northwest Forest Pass required/Hood River Ranger District, Mount Hood National Forest, (541) 352-6002
MAPS	USGS Mount Hood North; Green Trails Mount Hood 462
TRAIL NOTES	Leashed dogs okay

The Hike

Here's the granddaddy of all alpine hikes on the north side of Mount Hood, a climber's trail leading to incredible views and the north face routes up the glaciated 11,235-foot peak.

A climber's shelter stands just off the trail that climbs Cooper Spur.

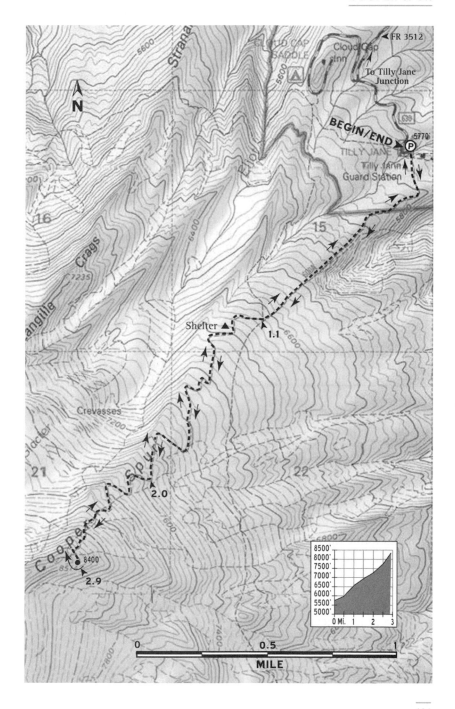

Getting There

Follow Interstate 84 east to Hood River and take Exit 64 to the four-way stop sign. Follow Highway 35 south for about 22 miles to Forest Road 3510, turn left and follow it about 2.5 miles to the Cooper Spur Inn and FR 3512, the Cooper Spur/Tilly Jane Road. Turn left on FR 3512 and follow it past a Sno-Park area and 9.5 bumpy miles to the Cloud Cap–Tilly Jane Campground Junction. Turn left and drive 0.5 mile to the Tilly Jane Campground. The trailhead is located at the southern end of the campground, past the ranger station, at 5,770 feet above sea level.

The Trail

Take plenty of film or digital storage for this hike and don't be duped into taking any panoramic photos until you are ready to collapse, out of breath, at your turnaround point. That needn't be the full 2.9 miles from the trailhead; just about any place above timberline will do. The view grows increasingly grand, to both those massive, snowy volcanoes to the north and the icy crags of Mount Hood above. Though every step leads to further oxygen depletion, you'll be tempted to take it.

Begin by crossing Tilly Jane Creek to a junction with Trail No. 643A, turn right, and climb on Trail No. 600A along the edge of the Polallie Creek canyon. At 1.1 miles, you'll strike the junction with Timberline Trail No. 600. Your route is up, up, up Trail No. 600B as it follows the spine of Cooper Spur.

Just past the junction, look to the right of the trail for the rock-walled Cooper Spur Shelter, a good spot to rest if it's windy or cold. Beyond the shelter, the trail gives no quarter as it switches back up the south side of Cooper Spur. The tread is mostly volcanic rock, sand, and gravel.

About 2.0 miles from the trailhead, hikers are likely to encounter a summer snowfield that may obliterate the trail, but route finding shouldn't be difficult. The path continues climbing the south side of Cooper Spur, eventually rounding a steep ridge to the south to a big rock climbers have dubbed "Tie-In Rock," 2.9 miles from the trailhead.

Sit. Look down on everything in northeastern Oregon and most of the western hemisphere. Look up to the blue ice and crevasses of the Eliot Glacier. Just try to catch your breath.

43. Lamberson Butte

RATING	🚶🚶🚶🚶
DISTANCE	6.8 miles round-trip
HIKING TIME	3.5 hours
ELEVATION GAIN	2,120 feet
HIGH POINT	7,280 feet
DIFFICULTY LEVEL	Moderately difficult
BEST SEASON	Fall, summer
PERMITS/CONTACT	Northwest Forest Pass required/Hood River Ranger District, Mount Hood National Forest, (541) 352-6002
MAPS	USGS Mount Hood North; Green Trails Mount Hood 462
TRAIL NOTES	Leashed dogs okay

The Hike

Here's another alpine stroll with splendid views across summer snowfields along Mount Hood's Timberline Trail, below the crevassed glaciers on the mountain's steep northeast face.

Getting There

Follow Interstate 84 east to Hood River and take Exit 64 to the four-way stop sign. Follow Highway 35 south for about 22 miles to Forest Road 3510, turn left and follow it about 2.5 miles to the Cooper Spur Inn and FR 3512, the Cooper Spur/Tilly Jane Road. Turn left on FR 3512 and follow it past a Sno-Park area and 9.5 bumpy miles to the Cloud Cap–Tilly Jane Campground Junction. Turn left and drive 0.5 mile to the Tilly Jane Campground. The trailhead is located at the southern end of the campground, past the ranger station, at 5,770 feet above sea level.

The Trail

Follow Trail No. 600A as it crosses Tilly Jane Creek and passes a junction with Trail No. 643A. Climb right on Trail No. 600A for 1.1 miles to a junction with Timberline Trail No. 600. Turn left on Trail No. 600 and follow it across rocky and—in summer—snowy ridges and gullies as it climbs underneath the icy east side of Mount Hood. This section of the trail is marked by log cairns that are easily seen

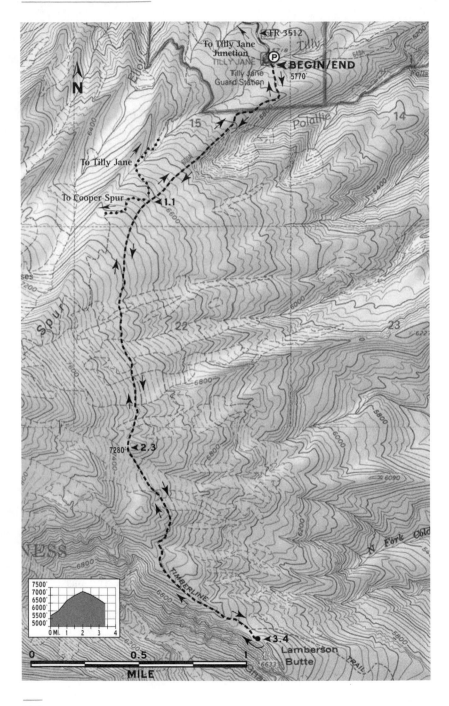

The trail to Lamberson Butte crosses barren volcanic slopes
and is marked by vertical poles.

on a clear fall day. But in summer fog, when sections of the trail
may still be snow-covered, navigating could be more difficult.

The trail climbs to about 7,300 feet above sea level, 2.3 miles
from the trailhead. This might be the best turnaround point for hikers with younger children, who won't want to climb back to this
high point. From the high point, the trail begins a descent across a
large summer snowfield and rounds a gullied ridge. It drops more
than 600 feet to the turnaround point, a 6,500-foot-high saddle
underneath Lamberson Butte and Gnarl Ridge, to the south.

44. Timberline Trail No. 600, West

RATING	🚶🚶🚶
DISTANCE	5.8 miles round-trip
HIKING TIME	3 hours
ELEVATION GAIN	550 feet
HIGH POINT	6,100 feet
DIFFICULTY LEVEL	Moderately difficult
BEST SEASON	Fall, summer
PERMITS/CONTACT	Northwest Forest Pass required/Hood River Ranger District, Mount Hood National Forest, (541) 352-6002
MAPS	USGS Mount Hood North; Green Trails Mount Hood 462
TRAIL NOTES	Leashed dogs okay; kid-friendly

The Hike

Save this trek for a day when Wy'east (Mount Hood) is shining in fall sunshine and late-blooming wildflowers are all around.

Getting There

Follow Interstate 84 east to Hood River and take Exit 64 to the four-way stop sign. Follow Highway 35 south for about 22 miles to Forest Road 3510, turn left and follow it about 2.5 miles to the Cooper Spur Inn and FR 3512, the Cooper Spur/Tilly Jane Road. Turn left on FR 3512 and follow it past a Sno-Park area and 9.5 bumpy miles to the Cloud Cap–Tilly Jane Campground Junction. Turn left and drive 0.5 mile to the Tilly Jane Campground. The trailhead is located at the southern end of the campground, past the ranger station, at 5,770 feet above sea level.

Day hikers with young children, or those wishing to shorten their round-trip walk by 0.8 mile, can turn right at the Cloud Cap–Tilly Jane Campground Junction. Drive 0.4 mile to the Cloud Cap Campground and hike 100 feet up the trail at the west end of the campground to the trailhead, 5,840 feet above sea level.

The Trail

You'll want to be in good shape to hike the Timberline Trail No. 600 from Tilly Jane Campground to a lateral moraine overlooking the

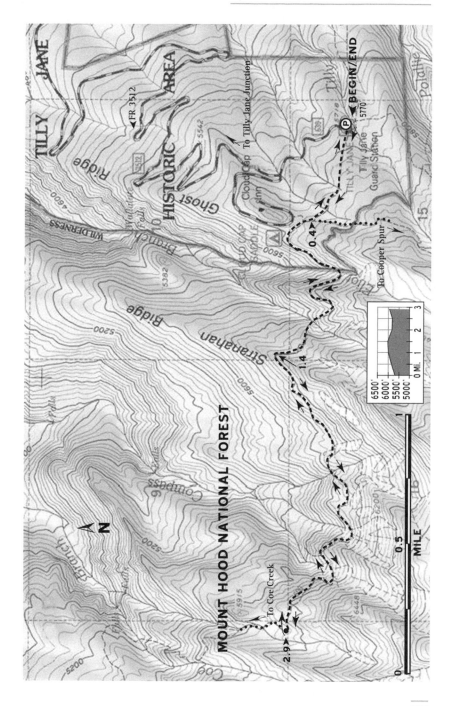

The Timberline Trail No. 600 to the west overlooks the Hood River Valley and the Columbia Gorge, with a view of Mount Adams through the fall haze.

Langille Glacier. It's not that the hills are long or steep, but you'll be consistently climbing or descending—more than a mile above sea level—as you traverse a number of gullies and creeks draining the Eliot and Langille Glaciers.

Begin by walking west through lichen-draped alpine evergreens on Trail No. 600A for **0.4** mile to a junction with Trail No. 600 at Cloud Cap Campground. It is a little-known fact that much of this lichen is pasted to the trees by a curious nocturnal creature, the Mount Hood Tufter. While few, if any, hikers have actually seen the Tufter at work, the male of this species decorates the tree trunks with green lichen in hopes of attracting a mate. Unfortunately, the female Tufter is blind as a bat at night and can't see the male's work. As you might guess, the species is on just about everybody's endangered species list. Feel free to check my research on this point.

The route seldom leaves alpine meadows and forest as it first drops into a gully crossing the Eliot Branch of the Middle Fork of Hood River. You'll climb out of the gully and round Stranhahan Ridge just below the Langille Crags, **1.4** miles from the trailhead.

Here's the high point of the hike and a good turnaround for families with young wilderness pedestrians.

To continue, follow the trail as it crosses several summer snowfields at the toe of the Langille Glacier. Here's where you'll get the best views of the mountain above and look north to Klickitat, the name Native Americans gave to Mount Adams. Beyond, the trail crosses a number of creeks that form the headwaters of Compass Creek before climbing to a sharp ridge at 5,900 feet at the western edge of the Langille Glacier. This is the turnaround point, 2.9 miles from the trailhead.

Going Farther

If you'd like a longer hike and a real workout, follow a way trail for 1.0 mile—or stay on the main Timberline Trail No. 600 for 1.2 miles—as they both descend steeply and join just above falls on Coe Creek. From there, climb again to stunning Elk Cove, an alpine meadow at the toe of the Coe Glacier. Round-trip to Elk Cove from Tilly Jane is 10.4 miles; from Cloud Cap, it's 9.6 miles.

Now, if you're up for a real trek, join the zanies who every summer attempt to do the entire 40.7 miles of Timberline Trail No. 600 around the mountain in one day! Surprisingly, many of them make it.

45. Polallie Ridge Loop

RATING	🚶🚶🚶
DISTANCE	4.4–5.8 miles round-trip
HIKING TIME	3 hours
ELEVATION GAIN	1,930 feet
HIGH POINT	5,770 feet
DIFFICULTY LEVEL	Moderately difficult
BEST SEASON	Fall, summer; open year-round
PERMITS/CONTACT	Northwest Forest Pass and Sno-Park Pass required/Hood River Ranger District, Mount Hood National Forest, (541) 352-6002
MAPS	USGS Mount Hood North; Green Trails Mount Hood 462
TRAIL NOTES	Leashed dogs okay; kid-friendly; winter cross-country ski trail

The Hike

This is a great walk in the summer and a fine cross-country ski or snowshoe loop in the winter, with views of Mount Hood, and wildflowers in the summer, and huckleberries in the fall.

Getting There

Follow Interstate 84 east to Hood River and take Exit 64 to the four-way stop sign. Follow Highway 35 south for about 22 miles to Forest Road 3510, turn left and follow it about 2.5 miles to the Cooper Spur Inn and FR 3512, the Cooper Spur/Tilly Jane Road. Turn left on FR 3512 and follow it past a Sno-Park area and 9.5 bumpy miles to the Cloud Cap–Tilly Jane Campground Junction. Turn left and drive 0.5 mile to the Tilly Jane Campground. The trailhead is located at the southern end of the campground, past the ranger station, at 5,770 feet above sea level. The winter trailhead is located at the Cooper Spur Sno-Park, at the junction of the road to Cooper Spur Ski Area and FR 3512, at 3,840 feet above sea level.

The Trail

Here's one of the very few hikes in this collection that begins by going downhill and ends, not surprisingly, by going uphill. Of course, in winter it's just the opposite for cross-country skiers.

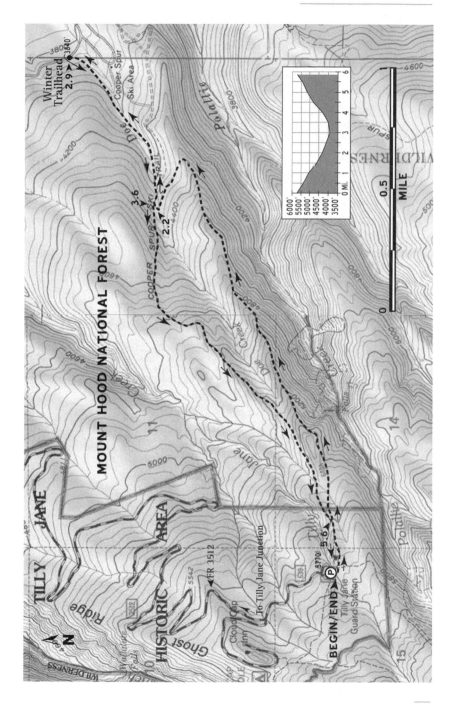

For the summer route, begin at Tilly Jane Campground and follow Trail No. 600 as it crosses Tilly Jane Creek to a junction with Trail No. 643A. Turn left here and descend through alpine forest for 0.2 mile to a junction with the Cooper Spur Ski Trail No. 643. Follow Trail No. 643A to the right as the path descends along the crest of the ridge past summer snowfields and falls on Polallie Creek, which rushes down the gully below the trail. The route continues down the crest of the ridge, mostly in forest, for nearly 2.0 miles before it turns sharply to the west and drops to a crossing of Doe Creek, 2.2 miles from the trailhead.

Just across Doe Creek, you'll strike the junction with Cooper Spur Trail No. 643. To shorten the hike by 1.4 miles, turn left here and follow Trail No. 643 back to its junction with Trail No. 643A and the trailhead. For the full 5.8-mile hike, turn right and follow Trail No. 643 as it descends above Doe Creek to the turnaround at the Cooper Spur Sno-Park Area, 2.9 miles from the trailhead. Climb back to the junction and stay right, following Trail No. 643 back to its junction with Trail No. 643A, at 5.6 miles, and continue the final 0.2 mile to the trailhead.

46. Bald Butte

RATING	🚶🚶🚶
DISTANCE	7.4 miles round-trip
HIKING TIME	4 hours
ELEVATION GAIN	2,020 feet
HIGH POINT	3,780 feet
DIFFICULTY LEVEL	Moderately difficult
BEST SEASON	Spring, fall
PERMITS/CONTACT	Northwest Forest Pass required/Hood River Ranger District, Mount Hood National Forest, (541) 352-6002
MAPS	USGS Parkdale; Green Trails Hood River 430
TRAIL NOTES	Leashed dogs okay; bikes allowed

The Hike

Here's a climb to splendid views of the Columbia River and Hood River Valley, with big snow giants all around and one—Mount Hood—so close that with binoculars you might spot climbers negotiating crevasses on the Eliot Glacier.

Getting There

Follow Highway 35 south from Hood River 14.2 miles to the Smullin Road, just south of Tollbridge County Park. Turn left and follow Smullin for 0.3 mile, where Smullin makes a 90-degree turn. Turn left at this corner onto a gravel road signed "Oak Ridge Trail 688-A." The parking area and trailhead are 200 feet up the road, 1,760 feet above sea level.

The Bald Butte Trail offers a good view of Mount Hood to the west.

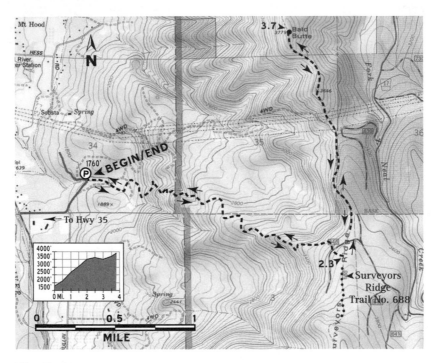

The Trail

Avoid this walk on hot summer days. It's a long, tough climb without an opportunity for those carrying filter bottles or pumps to replenish water.

The trail begins in what appears to be a clear-cut area with Bald Butte and power lines visible to the northeast. The open area eventually gives way to a forest of Oregon white oak as it climbs continually upward. The oak soon thins and yields to an open pine forest as the trail crosses a couple of old logging roads and ascends the crest of a ridge for **2.3** miles to a junction with Surveyors Ridge Trail No. 688. Turn left and follow that trail as it descends to cross a road and passes underneath power lines to a flat saddle, then begins a final climb to Bald Butte, the site of an old lookout, at **3.7** miles from the trailhead.

The often windy summit yields views of just about everything in Washington and Oregon, or seemingly so. Besides Mounts Hood and St. Helens, Mounts Rainier and Adams stretch from west to east.

47. Tamanawas Falls from Sherwood

RATING	🚶🚶🚶
DISTANCE	4.0 miles round-trip
HIKING TIME	2 hours
ELEVATION GAIN	480 feet
HIGH POINT	3,440 feet
DIFFICULTY LEVEL	Moderate
BEST SEASON	Fall, summer
PERMITS/CONTACT	Northwest Forest Pass required/Hood River Ranger District, Mount Hood National Forest, (541) 352-6002
MAPS	USGS Dog River; Green Trails Mount Hood 462
TRAIL NOTES	Leashed dogs okay; kid-friendly

The Hike

Just in case you didn't get your fill of waterfalls on the Columbia Gorge hikes, here's a short walk that is likely to be cooler than Gorge trails in the summer.

Tamanawas Falls viewpoint is reached via several trail options.

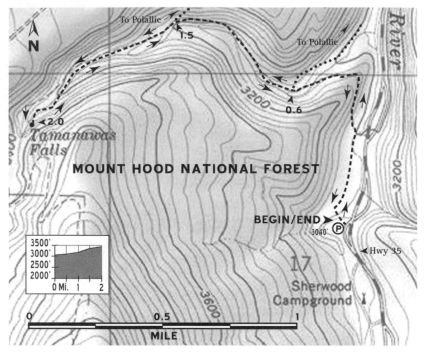

Getting There

Follow Interstate 84 east to Hood River and take Exit 64 to the four-way stop sign. Follow Highway 35 south for about 24 miles to a wide parking area at the highway curve just north of Sherwood Campground. Look for the trailhead sign near the middle of the parking area, 3,040 feet above sea level.

The Trail

Although likely to be crowded in the summer, this trail in late fall may well be yours and yours alone. It's a local favorite in summer for hikers looking to get above the heat and wind of the eastern Columbia Gorge.

Begin by crossing the East Fork of Hood River on a wide foot-bridge and immediately reach a junction with the Hood River Trail No. 650. Turn right and follow that trail as it gently drops through subalpine evergreen forest, then climbs to a steep slide area overlooking the highway and river. The trail turns at the overlook and drops gently to a footbridge crossing aptly named Cold Spring Creek. Just across the footbridge, 0.6 mile from the trailhead, you'll strike a junction with Trail No. 650A, which climbs up the East

Fork of Hood River from Polallie. Turn left and begin a pleasant climb along Cold Spring Creek, which tumbles over mossy rocks into clear pools below the trail.

At **1.5** miles from the trailhead, you'll arrive at a detour on Trail No. 645 around rock debris left by a massive slide. The main trail contours above the creek to its end at the turnaround point and a hillside view of Tamanawas Falls, **2.0** miles from the trailhead. The adventurous can scramble across a steep, slippery rocky slope to the cliff overhang behind the waterfall.

Going Farther

Sherwood Campground, a Mount Hood National Forest campground just upstream from the Tamanawas Falls trailhead, offers pleasant sites that provide a quiet alternative to the Oregon State Park campgrounds in the Columbia Gorge along I-84 and the Union Pacific Railroad. Both Sherwood and Robinhood Campgrounds, upstream, make good bases for hikes along the Highway 35 corridor.

A hiker crosses Hood River near Sherwood Campground
on the way to Tamanawas Falls.

48. Tamanawas Falls Loop

RATING	🚶🚶🚶
DISTANCE	5.8 miles round-trip
HIKING TIME	3 hours
ELEVATION GAIN	740 feet
HIGH POINT	3,600 feet
DIFFICULTY LEVEL	Moderate
BEST SEASON	Fall, summer
PERMITS/CONTACT	Northwest Forest Pass required/Hood River Ranger District, Mount Hood National Forest, (541) 352-6002
MAPS	USGS Dog River; Green Trails Mount Hood 462
TRAIL NOTES	Leashed dogs okay

The Hike

This is a second, slightly longer loop hike to Tamanawas Falls, requiring a little more muscle power and likely to be less crowded in summer for several miles.

Getting There

Follow Interstate 84 east to Hood River and take Exit 64 to the four-way stop sign. Follow Highway 35 south for about 24 miles to a wide parking area at the highway curve just north of Sherwood Campground. Look for the trailhead sign near the middle of the parking area, 3,040 feet above sea level.

The Trail

You'll begin this hike at the trailhead just below Sherwood Campground, and follow the route described for Tamanawas Falls from Sherwood (see hike #47). Cross the footbridge and turn north along the East Fork of Hood River on Trail No. 650. The route downstream climbs gently to an overlook of the river and highway, then turns and descends to a footbridge crossing of Cold Spring Creek.

Cross the bridge and turn left at the junction with Trail No. 650A, 0.6 mile from the trailhead. This trail climbs gently along Cold Spring Creek for 0.9 mile. In the fall, sparkling pools of the creek are accented by green mosses and bright fall leaves.

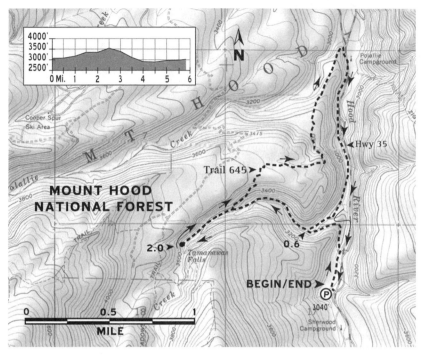

At **1.5** miles, you'll switchback sharply just under cliffs and begin a detour on Trail No. 645. Climb steeply for a hundred feet or so and look to the left for the rough trail through the debris of a slide that wiped out the trail. Traverse above the creek to the turnaround and viewpoint of Tamanawas Falls, **2.0** miles from the trailhead. Some hikers scramble across the rocky slope to an alcove behind the falls.

To return, follow the trail back to Trail No. 645 and follow it to the left as it climbs underneath cliffs to a broad forested ridge and intersects trails up Cold Spring Creek and Bluegrass Ridge. Stay right and begin a steep descent that switches back, passes an overlook above damage from a 1980 flood, and drops in 1.2 miles to a junction with the East Fork Trail No. 650, just across Highway 35 from Polallie Campground.

Stay right at the junction and begin a gentle climb along the banks of the East Fork for 1.0 mile to the junction with Trail No. 650A to close the loop. Turn left across the footbridge, climb and drop along the river to the East Fork footbridge and trailhead.

49. Horsethief Meadows

RATING	🥾🥾🥾
DISTANCE	8.8 miles round-trip
HIKING TIME	4 hours
ELEVATION GAIN	550 feet
HIGH POINT	3,550 feet
DIFFICULTY LEVEL	Moderate
BEST SEASON	Fall, summer
PERMITS/CONTACT	Northwest Forest Pass required/Hood River Ranger District, Mount Hood National Forest, (541) 352-6002
MAPS	USGS Dog River; Green Trails Mount Hood 462
TRAIL NOTES	Leashed dogs okay; kid-friendly

The Hike

This is a pleasant walk through a subalpine forest along the East Fork of Hood River between two U.S. Forest Service campgrounds, little used in the fall.

Getting There

Follow Interstate 84 east to Hood River and take Exit 64 to the four-way stop sign. Follow Highway 35 south for about 24 miles to a wide parking area at the highway curve just north of Sherwood Campground. Look for the trailhead sign near the middle of the parking area, 3,040 feet above sea level.

The Trail

Here's a hike best saved for those fall days when the view might be obscured by clouds and fog. In the late fall it makes a splendid first-snow walk in the forest.

Begin by crossing the East Fork of Hood River on a footbridge. Just across the bridge, you'll intersect the East Fork Trail No. 650. Turn left and follow the trail through forest beside the river past Sherwood Campground on the opposite side of the river. The route continues to climb gently—but for the length of the hike it would rate as "Easy"—along the river in forested flatland, crossing several streams that tumble from Bluegrass Ridge

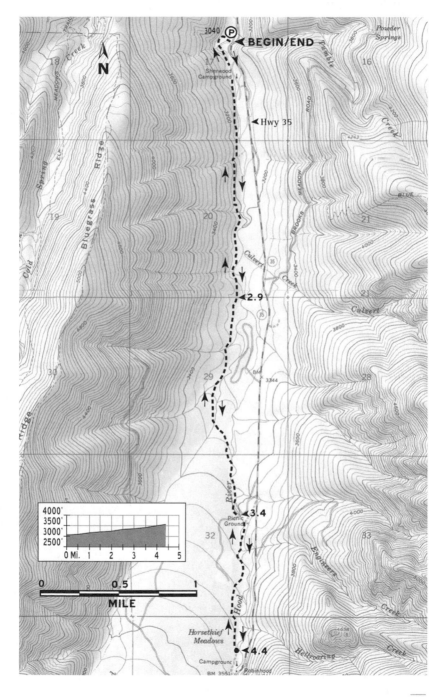

to the west. At **2.9** miles, you'll pass river flats just across the river from Culvert Creek and Highway 35, a good turnaround for families with younger children.

Beyond, the trail climbs past three branches of Robinhood Creek, cuts through a picnic area **3.4** miles from the trailhead, and meanders through a clearing at Horsethief Meadows, the turnaround point **4.4** miles from the trailhead.

50. Lookout Mountain (Hard Way)

RATING	🚶🚶🚶🚶🚶
DISTANCE	7.0 miles round-trip
HIKING TIME	4 hours
ELEVATION GAIN	2,100 feet
HIGH POINT	6,525 feet
DIFFICULTY LEVEL	Moderately difficult
BEST SEASON	Summer
PERMITS/CONTACT	None/Mount Hood National Forest, (541) 467-2291
MAPS	USGS Badger Lake; Green Trails Mount Hood
TRAIL NOTES	Leashed dogs okay

The Hike

The vista from Lookout Mountain is difficult to beat anywhere in the Columbia Gorge or surrounding territory, and well worth hiking the Hard Way trail to get there.

Getting There

From Hood River, drive 26.5 miles south on Highway 35 to a junction with Forest Road 44 and turn left. Follow the paved FR 44 for 8.6 miles to Forest Road 4420, on the right. Turn right on this paved road and follow it for 4.4 miles, passing Fifteenmile Campground (a good primitive base camp for this hike and hike #52), to the Fret Creek Trailhead, 4,500 feet above sea level.

The Trail

Masochistic hikers will be pleased to know that there is an even harder way to get to Lookout Mountain—but you won't read about it here. Instead, slip on the Vibrams, find the Fret Creek Trail 456A on the opposite side of the road from the parking area, and begin a fairly steep climb on a rounded ridge about the creek. The forest understory here is crowded with huckleberry bushes, although they didn't look like they'd produce much fruit in August 2010.

Just about the time you warm up to the steep climb, the grade eases a bit 0.5 mile from the trailhead, and you'll cross Fret Creek on a plank bridge the first of three times. During the next mile, you'll face a moderate climb through a forest that grows increasingly open. The trail meanders up wide ridges on either side of the creek to the last crossing on boulders, where you'll begin climbing more steeply again.

The forest opens at **2.0** miles from the trailhead and you'll pass a short side trail on the left leading down to shallow Oval Lake, which might make a good spot to cool off on your return. Just beyond, **2.2** miles from the trailhead, you'll reach a junction with Divide Trail 458.

Turn right here and follow the Divide Trail as it snakes under the top of a precipitous, rocky ridge that plunges to the south into the Badger Creek Wilderness and valley. Crest the ridge where, on clear days, you'll see Mount Jefferson to the south. The trail alternately climbs and descends in short chunks for 1 mile, passing a helicopter landing site and, **3.3** miles from the trailhead, coming to Senecal Spring, which appears to be the source of Fifteenmile Creek. A short side trail leads to the spring.

Beyond, the trail gets steeper as it ascends through forest to the rocky, open summit of Lookout Mountain. The view in every

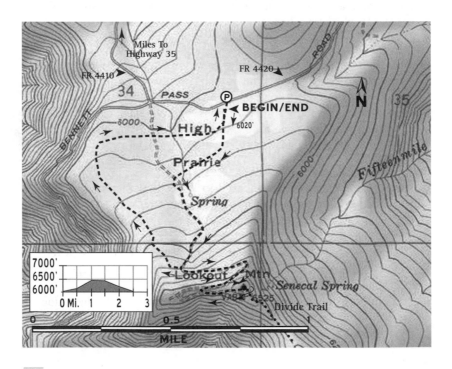

Mount Hood towers above meadows along the Lookout Mountain Trail.

direction is spectacular, from the dry plains of eastern Oregon to the snowy summits of the Cascade Mountains. The rocky, icy east face of Mount Hood appears close enough that you might hear the crunch and rumble of the Elliot or White glaciers as they grind away at the mountain.

51. Lookout Mountain (Easy Way)

RATING	🚶🚶🚶🚶🚶
DISTANCE	2.5 miles round-trip
HIKING TIME	1.5 hours
ELEVATION GAIN	600 feet
HIGH POINT	6,525 feet
DIFFICULTY LEVEL	Easy
BEST SEASON	Summer
PERMITS/CONTACT	Northwest Forest Pass required/ Mount Hood National Forest, (541) 352-6002
MAPS	USGS Badger Lake; Green Trails Mount Hood
TRAIL NOTES	Leashed dogs okay

The Easy Way to Lookout Mountain is a wide, gentle path.

The Hike

This is the short, pleasant way to get the great view from Lookout Mountain. (Refer to the map on page 154 for this trail.)

Getting There

From Hood River, drive 26.5 miles south on Highway 35 to a junction with Forest Road 44 and turn left. Follow the paved FR 44 for 3.8 miles and turn right on Forest Road 4410. This gravel road climbs past junctions with several smaller, less well-used roads for 4.7 miles to a T intersection with the High Prairie Road 4420 to the left and Forest Road 3550 on the right. Turn left on the High Prairie Road and drive 200 yards to the trailhead on the left, where you'll find a restroom and plenty of parking. The High Prairie Trail 493 to Lookout Mountain begins across the road, 6,020 feet above sea level.

The Trail

You couldn't find a better spot to begin a short climb to an excellent mountain vista. Green alpine meadows pocked with deer and elk tracks spread between alpine fir and peekaboo views of Mount Hood to the west. Don't feel guilty about not looking; you can't miss Wy'east from the summit of Lookout Mountain.

The main trail to the summit is always the widest of several side trails, and makes a couple of round switchbacks before joining the Divide Trail 458 just below the summit. Turn left and follow the Divide Trail to the summit. You can make a short loop on the return by following a horse trail to its junction with the main trail, just above the trailhead.

Shooting stars fill the meadows along the trails to Lookout Mountain.

52. Palisade Point

RATING	 ...
DISTANCE	4.6 miles round-trip
HIKING TIME	2.5 hours
ELEVATION GAIN	1,320 feet
HIGH POINT	5,822 feet
DIFFICULTY LEVEL	Moderate
BEST SEASON	Summer
PERMITS/CONTACT	None/Mount Hood National Forest (541) 467-2291
MAPS	USGS Badger Lake; Green Trails Mount Hood
TRAIL NOTES	Leashed dogs okay

Rock turrets stand guard above the Badger Creek Wilderness at Palisade Point.

The Hike

This trail passes tiny Oval Lake and follows the high, scenic Divide Trail along the crest of a rocky alpine ridge with views across eastern and southern Oregon.

Getting There

From Hood River, drive 26.5 miles south on Highway 35 to a junction with Forest Road 44 and turn left. Follow the paved FR 44 for 8.6 miles to Forest Road 4420, on the right. Turn right on this paved road and follow it for 4.4 miles, passing Fifteenmile Campground (a good primitive base camp for this hike and hike #50), to the Fret Creek Trailhead, 4,500 feet above sea level.

The Trail

This hike shares the same route with the trail to Lookout Mountain (Hard Way) for 2.1 miles; see hike #50. Climb on Fret Creek Trail 456A past Oval Lake to its junction with Divide Trail 458.

Turn left at the junction and in a few hundred yards, cross a rocky open area to a steep switchback and climb to the crest of the

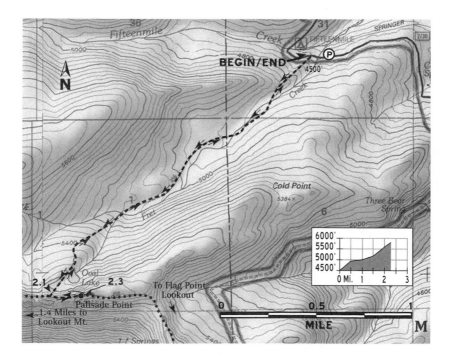

ridge. The trail winds along the ridge 0.3 mile from the junction to 5,822-foot-high Palisade Point, with its great vista to the south and east. For a real thrill, scramble to the rocky peak and look down about 350 vertical feet to the Badger Creek Wilderness.

Going Farther

For a longer walk, you can take the Divide Trail for another 1.4 miles to the road leading to Flag Point Lookout, then follow the road another 0.5 mile to the lookout.

53. Lost Lake Loop

RATING 𝕏 𝕏 𝕏
DISTANCE 3.2 miles round-trip
HIKING TIME 1 hour
ELEVATION GAIN 40 feet
HIGH POINT 3,180 feet
DIFFICULTY LEVEL Easy
BEST SEASON Late fall, summer
PERMITS/CONTACT Lost Lake Resort parking fee or
Northwest Forest Pass required/Hood
River Ranger District, Mount Hood
National Forest, (541) 352-6002
MAPS USGS Bull Run Lake; Green Trails
Government Camp 461
TRAIL NOTES Leashed dogs okay; kid-friendly

The Hike

Late fall is the best time for this easy walk, when the crowds have thinned. Hikers who have been here on clear days allege that the view of Mount Hood from Lost Lake is fantastic.

Getting There

From Portland, follow Interstate 84 to Hood River, Exit 62. Turn right and drive east to 13th Street. Turn right on 13th and drive uphill through the Hood River Heights business district as 13th merges into Tucker Road. Stay on Tucker as it makes three 90-degree turns, the final being a left turn at Windmaster Corner. Continue following Tucker Road 8 miles to the Dee Highway intersection, then turn right past the old Dee mill, and turn left on Lost Lake Road, following it 13.7 curving miles to Lost Lake, at 3,140 feet above sea level.

Hikers from Sandy and perhaps Gresham may follow Highway 26 to Zigzag and follow Forest Road 18 over Lolo Pass to FR 13, turning left and following it 6.5 miles to Lost Lake.

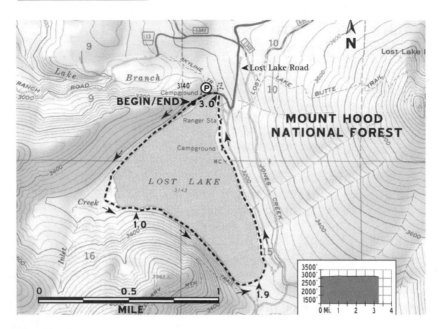

The Trail

Mother Nature sometimes doles out cruel and unusual punishment, as she did to me while I tried to photograph Mount Hood from a splendid viewpoint purported to be along the Lost Lake Trail. But you will not hear raves from me about the view, because all I saw on three visits to beautiful Lost Lake was rain, fog, and big puffy clouds.

It rained so hard on my first visit to Lost Lake that I inadvertently stomped on three rainbow trout that appeared to be swimming around the Lost Lake Trail No. 656, which circles the lake. On my second visit, I raced west on I-84 from an overnight camp at Deschutes River Recreation Area, ogling Wy'east as it sparkled in morning sunshine above The Dalles. But by the time I reached the lake, the mountain had ducked behind clouds and the wind whipped the lake to a white froth. On my third visit, clouds again intervened and I spent the day climbing up to Lost Lake Butte, which I propose renaming Lost View Butte.

This fine, gentle loop hike is best done from the North Day Use trailhead, closest to the supposed Mount Hood viewpoint. Walk west for **1.0** mile to the southwestern end of the lake, climbing and dropping through evergreen forest. At **1.9** miles, you'll reach

Rain clouds hide the view of Mount Hood at Lost Lake.

the south end of the lake and a junction with Huckleberry Mountain Trail No. 617. Stay left here and follow the trail north along the shore below the campground loops, boat ramp, and barrier-free fishing dock. Cross the outlet stream at 3.0 miles and walk the road or shore trail 0.2 mile to the trailhead.

Going Farther

Lost Lake Resort rents rowboats, canoes, and paddle boats. There's a general store and rustic cabins for rent. The Forest Service campground is usually full by Thursday or Friday in summer but less crowded after Labor Day.

54. Lost Lake Butte

RATING	🥾🥾🥾🥾
DISTANCE	3.8 miles round-trip
HIKING TIME	3 hours
ELEVATION GAIN	1,300 feet
HIGH POINT	4,468 feet
DIFFICULTY LEVEL	Moderately difficult
BEST SEASON	Fall, summer
PERMITS/CONTACT	Lost Lake Resort parking fee or Northwest Forest Pass required/Hood River Ranger District, Mount Hood National Forest, (541) 352-6002
MAPS	USGS Bull Run Lake; Green Trails Government Camp 461
TRAIL NOTES	Leashed dogs okay

The Hike

This moderately strenuous climb leads through subalpine forest to an expansive view of the snowy giants to the north, the lake below, and—so others claim—Mount Hood just a shout away.

Getting There

From Portland, follow Interstate 84 to Hood River, Exit 62. Turn right and drive east to 13th Street. Turn right on 13th and drive uphill through the Hood River Heights business district as 13th merges into Tucker Road. Stay on Tucker as it makes three 90-degree turns, the final being a left turn at Windmaster Corner. Continue following Tucker Road 8 miles to the Dee Highway intersection,

A fall morning at Lost Lake lacks summer crowds.

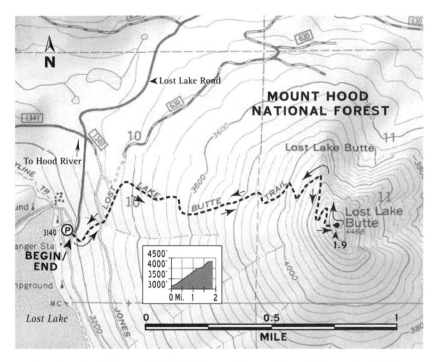

then turn right past the old Dee mill, and turn left on Lost Lake Road, following it 13.7 curving miles to Lost Lake, at 3,140 feet above sea level.

Hikers from Sandy and perhaps Gresham may follow Highway 26 to Zigzag and follow Forest Road 18 over Lolo Pass to Lost Lake Road, turning left and following it 6.5 miles to Lost Lake.

The Trail

You can begin this hike from the day-use parking area near the general store. Lost Lake Butte Trail No. 616 climbs east, crossing the campground road before reaching a junction at 0.2 mile with Skyline Trail No. 655. Continue straight, uphill past the junction in the forest, through what must be spectacular rhododendron displays in late spring or early summer.

The trail climbs in steep switchbacks 1,300 feet in 1.9 miles, making the final ascent on the north side of the butte, where the view from an old lookout site opens in all directions—according to hikers who have been there on days when fog didn't cloak the summit like a giant cotton ball. To the north is Mount Adams, with Rainier in the distance. Mount Hood lies to the south.

55. Huckleberry Mountain Trail

RATING	🚶🚶🚶
DISTANCE	6.0 miles round-trip
HIKING TIME	3 hours
ELEVATION GAIN	1,200 feet
HIGH POINT	4,350 feet
DIFFICULTY LEVEL	Moderately difficult
BEST SEASON	Late summer, fall
PERMITS/CONTACT	Lost Lake Resort parking fee or Northwest Forest Pass required/Hood River Ranger District, Mount Hood National Forest, (541) 352-6002
MAPS	USGS Bull Run Lake; Green Trails Government Camp 461
TRAIL NOTES	Leashed dogs okay

The Hike

Climb along this trail in the fall, when the bushes yield fruit so tasty and lush you may never reach the turnaround point.

Getting There

From Portland, follow Interstate 84 to Hood River, Exit 62. Turn right and drive east to 13th Street. Turn right on 13th and drive uphill through the Hood River Heights business district as 13th merges into Tucker Road. Stay on Tucker as it makes three 90-degree turns, the final being a left turn at Windmaster Corner. Continue following Tucker Road 8 miles to the Dee Highway intersection, then turn right past the old Dee mill, and turn left on Lost Lake Road, following it 13.7 curving miles to Lost Lake, at 3,140 feet above sea level.

Hikers from Sandy and perhaps Gresham may follow Highway 26 to Zigzag and follow Forest Road 18 over Lolo Pass to Lost Lake Road, turning left and following it 6.5 miles to Lost Lake.

After passing the entrance kiosk, drive south past the campground loops and group camps to the gated Jones Creek Road. Turn right on the gravel Sentinel Spur Road and drive 0.2 mile to the trailhead on the right, 3,165 feet above sea level.

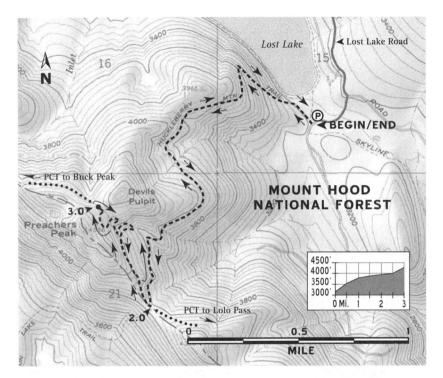

The Trail

Don't believe the sign at the trailhead, which identifies it as the trail to Lost Lake. You'll find an immediate junction with the Huckleberry Mountain Trail No. 617, which forks to the left and begins climbing in rhododendron glades and old evergreen forest above Lost Lake. You'll climb about **0.4** mile, then switchback continuing through old forest and rhododendrons. The understory gradually yields to the tasty berries that give this trail its name and makes this a delicious early fall excursion (which may slow your uphill pace!).

At **1.2** miles, it rounds a basin at the headwaters of Jones Creek underneath the Devil's Pulpit and reaches a junction with the Pacific Crest Trail 2000, located at 4,180 feet above sea level, at **2.0** miles. Turn right on the PCT and climb to the turnaround point, a forested saddle between Devil's Pulpit and Preacher's Peak, **3.0** miles from the trailhead.

Huckleberry Mountain Trail is lined by rhododendrons
in spring and blueberries in fall.

Going Farther

For more exercise, the trail continues past the turnaround point
and follows the 4,200-foot ridge to a second saddle at 4,480 feet,
just south of Buck Peak. Just east of the saddle, look for the Buck
Peak way trail leading right, 3.8 miles from the trailhead. Turn
right and climb under the peak from the north, then switchback
and climb steeply to the summit, 4,751 feet above sea level and 4.2
miles from the trailhead. You'll get peekaboo views of Mount Hood
and Mount Adams.

MOUNT ADAMS SOUTH

Summer and fall are prime hiking seasons at this snowcapped volcano.

MOUNT ADAMS SOUTH

I first visited the sunny southern slopes of Mount Adams for summer skiing in the late 1970s, climbing above Cold Springs to carve ragged smiles in the snow with the Trout Lake locals. I remember that one guy bolted his three-pin bindings to his old downhill skis via holes drilled all the way through the ski. The trails haven't changed much, although I would swear they've gotten longer and steeper in the past four decades.

Save the pathways on the southern slopes of Mount Adams and in the Wind River area for the summer and fall, after the roads to the high trailheads are free of snow. The popular hikes—those that follow the South Climb route on Adams and to Racetrack—can be frightfully crowded in the summer and absolutely lonesome for feet in late fall.

I ran into a Forest Service ranger on one of the hikes along the South Climb route who made an interesting observation. "I think Oregon residents don't know there's a mountain over here," she said. "All I see are people from Washington." Perhaps it's the seventy-five-cent toll on the Hood River Bridge. Anyway, here's the deal: Oregon hikers are more than welcome on Mount Adams, as long as Washington hikers can leave their boot prints on Mount Hood.

Sunshine is a frequent companion on the southern side of Adams because of its easterly location above the Columbia Gorge. Mount St. Helens (Loo-Wit to Native Americans) stretches to the west and, despite her lower stance since 1980, still blocks some of the rain clouds headed for Adams. When the sky is blue, climb high on the mountain; when the clouds cover the summit, look for walks in the forest.

56. Bird Creek Meadows

RATING	🚶🚶🚶
DISTANCE	7.0 miles round-trip
HIKING TIME	3.5 hours
ELEVATION GAIN	950 feet
HIGH POINT	6,300 feet
DIFFICULTY LEVEL	Moderate
BEST SEASON	Summer, fall
PERMITS/CONTACT	Northwest Forest Pass required/ Mount Adams Ranger District, (509) 395-3400
MAPS	USGS Mount Adams West; Green Trails Mount Adams West 366
TRAIL NOTES	Leashed dogs okay; kid-friendly

The Hike

The trek to Bird Creek Meadows provides splendid views, alpine wildflowers, and big summer snowfields to keep you cool on hot summer days. A car-key exchange and one-way walk is possible from Bird Lake.

Getting There

From Trout Lake, drive north at the Y intersection on Forest Road 23 for 1.3 miles to its junction with FR 80, bear right on FR 80 and drive 4.3 miles to a junction with FR 8040. Keep right on FR 8040 for 5.2 miles to Morrison Creek, bear right and follow FR 8040-500 for 2.8 miles to the trailhead at Cold Springs, 5,600 feet above sea level.

The Trail

This fine alpine walk climbs in pine forests up the sunny southern slopes of 12,276-foot Mount Adams, a beautiful volcano that cups summer snowfields in its nooks and canyons well into mid-July. You'll be joined for the first 1.2 miles of the trail with climbers bound for the popular South Climb route—but you'll likely have less company on the rest of the hike.

The first mile of this climb is the steepest, following an old abandoned road to a trail junction and the old Timberline Campground.

When summer snow covers Bird Creek Meadows,
follow the log cairns beside the path.

This route was once used by pack trains that climbed all the way to
the summit of Mount Adams. It climbs through increasingly open
pine forest to the junction with the Round-the-Mountain Trail No.
9 at **1.2** miles. Here the forest turns to alpine meadows, with awesome views of the mountain above and south across the White
Salmon River valley and Columbia Gorge to Mount Hood.

Turn right on the Round-the-Mountain Trail and follow it for 2.3
miles to beautiful Bird Creek Meadows. You'll cross a number of
wide snowfields that linger far into July, but the trail is easily fol-
lowed in good weather as it meanders up and down at timberline.
About **2.2** miles from the trailhead, you'll cross the top portion of
the Aiken Lava Bed, all crumpled basalt flowing like a rock river to
the south. The trail descends briefly to cross the rocks, then climbs
back to an alpine pine forest to cross the marked boundary with the
Yakama Indian Reservation. Just beyond, cross the first of several
creeks in the meadows to a junction with the Gotchen Creek Trail,
an ideal picnic spot and turnaround at **3.5** miles from the trailhead.

Going Farther

For a one-way hike and car-key exchange, or for hikers leaving
an auto at Bird Lake, continue on the Round-the-Mountain Trail
for 0.4 mile to a junction with Crooked Creek Trail. Turn right and
descend to Bird Lake on the Yakama Reservation, about 8 miles up
Forest Road 82 from its junction with FR 80.

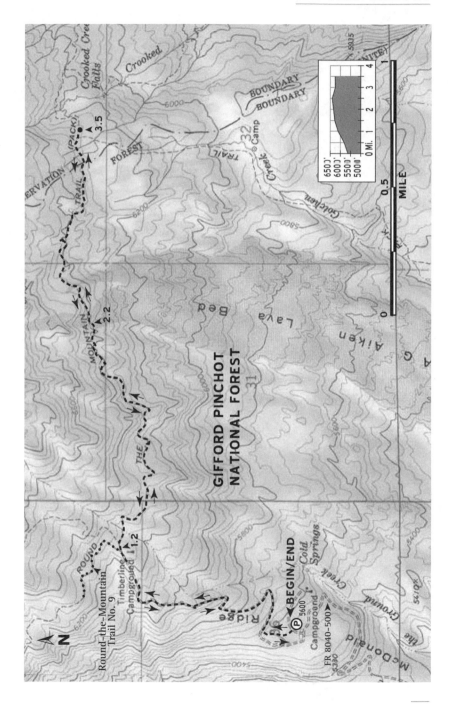

BIRD CREEK MEADOWS

Crooked Creek Falls

Crooked Creek

Crooked

BOUNDARY

BOUNDARY

FOREST

RESERVATION

TRAIL (PACK)

3.5

32

Camp

Golchen Creek

TRAIL

GRANITE

5935

6000

5800

5800

2.2

MOUNTAIN

Lava Bed

Aiken

GIFFORD PINCHOT
NATIONAL FOREST

31

THE

5600

1.2

ROUND

Timberline
Campground

Campground

Round-the-Mountain
Trail No. 9

N

BEGIN/END

Cold Springs

P

5600

Campground

FR 8040-500

5400

5400

the (Ground)

McDonald

Creek

5403

0   0.5   1   MILE

650'
600'
550'
500'

0 Mi. 1 2 3 4

175

57. Crescent Glacier

RATING	 🚶🚶🚶🚶
DISTANCE	6.8 miles round-trip
HIKING TIME	4 hours
ELEVATION GAIN	2,400 feet
HIGH POINT	8,000 feet
DIFFICULTY LEVEL	Difficult
BEST SEASON	Summer, fall
PERMITS/CONTACT	Northwest Forest Pass and free Wilderness Use Permit required/ Mount Adams Ranger District, (509) 395-3400
MAPS	USGS Mount Adams West; Green Trails Mount Adams West 366
TRAIL NOTES	Leashed dogs okay

The Hike

You'll have company on this hike most any time during the summer, when hundreds of mountaineers tackle the southern route up Mount Adams. Don't let that deter you from enjoying one of the most scenic alpine hikes in Washington state.

Mountaineers follow the Crescent Glacier Trail on the South Climb route of Mount Adams.

Getting There

From Trout Lake, drive north at the Y intersection on Forest Road 23 for 1.3 miles to its junction with FR 80, bear right on FR 80 and drive 4.3 miles to a junction with FR 8040. Keep right on FR 8040 for 5.2 miles to Morrison Creek, bear right and follow FR 8040-500 for 2.8 miles to the trailhead at Cold Springs, 5,600 feet above sea level.

The Trail

This is a no-nonsense climb up Mount Adams to a camp and seasonal ranger camp beside a real, live glacier. Those who don't wish to purchase a Cascade Volcano Pass ($15–$30 in 2010) should plan to turn around at the 7,000-foot level, a 5.0-mile round-trip hike from the trailhead.

Begin by following the old abandoned road to Timberline Campground as it climbs 1.2 miles from the trailhead. You'll follow the trail through sparse pine forest as it climbs to a junction with the Round-the-Mountain Trail No. 9. Hikers who don't plan to climb above the 7,000-foot level should issue themselves a Wilderness Use Permit at this junction.

To continue, climb north toward the rock and ice on the south face of 12,276-foot Mount Adams. The route alternately passes through pines twisted by frequent winds and snow and volcanic meadows to summer snowfields that are the headwaters of Morrison Creek, 6,800 feet above sea level. From this point, the route abandons mundane switchbacks and begins a long, steady climb toward the Crescent Glacier above. About 2.5 miles from the trailhead, you'll climb to 7,000 feet. If you plan to continue, pack along a Cascades Volcano Pass, available at the Trout Lake Ranger Station; otherwise, this makes an excellent picnic spot and turnaround point.

The trail continues to climb in increasingly steep gulps to a camp along the west side of the Crescent Glacier, 3.4 miles from the trailhead. A seasonal ranger camp is located here in summer.

Going Farther

Hikers with route-finding experience can continue to climb on a well-trod snow or rock path to Lunch Counter, a flat saddle below a massive snow- and icefield at about 9,100 feet above sea level. This is a popular climbers' camp for mountaineers headed to the summit.

58. Crofton Ridge

RATING	🥾🥾🥾
DISTANCE	7.8 miles round-trip
HIKING TIME	4 hours
ELEVATION GAIN	720 feet
HIGH POINT	6,225 feet
DIFFICULTY LEVEL	Moderately difficult
BEST SEASON	Summer, fall
PERMITS/CONTACT	Northwest Forest Pass and free Wilderness Use Permit required/ Mount Adams Ranger District, (509) 395-3400
MAPS	USGS Mount Adams West; Green Trails Mount Adams West 366
TRAIL NOTES	Leashed dogs okay

The Hike

This walk offers just about everything you might want in an alpine stroll: wildflower-filled meadows, mind-melting vistas, and summer-lingering snowfields. Hikers with two cars have a one-way option with a key exchange.

Getting There

From Trout Lake, drive north at the Y intersection on Forest Road 23 for 1.3 miles to its junction with FR 80, bear right on FR 80 and drive 4.3 miles to a junction with FR 8040. Keep right on FR 8040 for 5.2 miles to Morrison Creek, bear right and follow FR 8040-500 for 2.8 miles to the trailhead at Cold Springs, 5,600 feet above sea level.

The Trail

You'll begin this hike on the crowded South Climb Trail No. 183, the most popular route among climbers headed for 12,276-foot Mount Adams. The trail, once an old road, climbs steadily but never too steeply for 1.2 miles through pine forest that grows increasingly thinner as you climb.

At 1.2 miles, you'll strike a junction with the South Climb Trail and the Round-the-Mountain Trail No. 9. Here the views open to Crescent Glacier and Mount Adams to the north. Turn left on the

The Round-the-Mountain Trail No. 9 heads west from the
junction with the Crescent Glacier Trail.

Round-the-Mountain Trail and wander through alpine forest and
meadows, crossing shaded snowfields that may linger through July.
Views through the pines to the south include the White Salmon
River valley and Mount Hood.

You'll cross Morrison Creek 1.9 miles from the trailhead, a good
source of water in early summer for those with filter pumps or bottles. The route climbs briefly out of the creek canyon, then drops
steeply about 200 feet, rounds a sharp ridge, and climbs around a

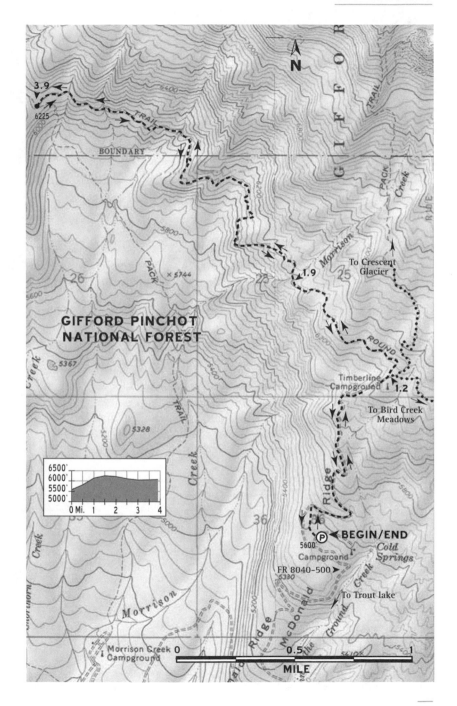

Snowmelt creeks ripple through marsh marigold meadows
on the Round-the-Mountain Trail 9 at Mount Adams.

wide gully to cross several seasonal creeks. After about 2 miles,
you'll reach a flat saddle and junction with the Crofton Creek Trail
No. 16. This is your turnaround point.

Going Farther

Hiking parties with two cars can plan a key exchange with hikers
who climb up Crofton Creek Trail No. 16 for 2.8 miles to the Round-
the-Mountain Trail junction. Total one-way distance for this option
would be 6.7 miles. The Crofton Creek trailhead is located off
Forest Road 8061 at Shorthorn.

59. Salt Creek Trail

RATING	🚶🚶
DISTANCE	7.6 miles round-trip
HIKING TIME	4 hours
ELEVATION GAIN	580 feet
HIGH POINT	3,640 feet
DIFFICULTY LEVEL	Moderate
BEST SEASON	Summer, fall
PERMITS/CONTACT	Northwest Forest Pass and free Wilderness Use Permit required/ Mount Adams Ranger District, (509) 395-3400
MAPS	USGS Mount Adams West; Green Trails Mount Adams West 366
TRAIL NOTES	Leashed dogs okay; kid-friendly

The Hike

Save this forest walk for a cloudy or rainy day when views aren't important or shade is welcome on a hot summer day. This makes a great walk for hikers who prefer greater solitude than that found on more popular Mount Adams trails.

Salt Creek Trail passes several beaver ponds and is a good forest walk in rainy or foggy weather.

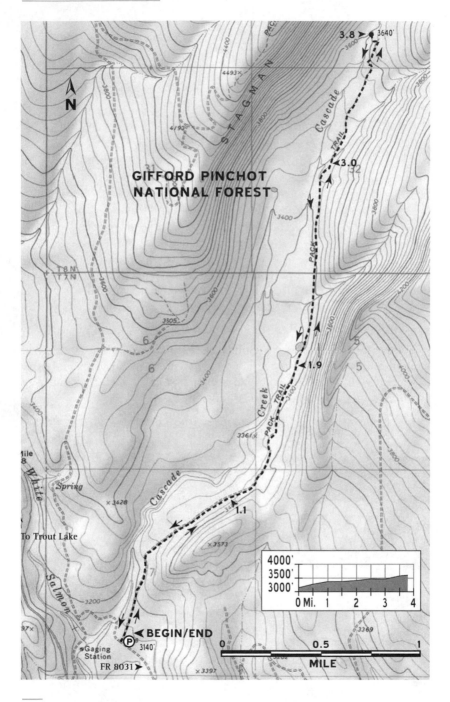

Getting There

From Trout Lake, drive north at the Y intersection on Forest Road 23 for 1.2 miles to its junction with FR 80, bear left on FR 23 for 7.9 miles to its junction with FR 8031. Turn right and drive 0.7 mile to the trailhead, passing the junction with FR 8031-070 to the right at 0.4 mile. The first mile of this hike is along FR 8031-060, which is closed to motorized vehicles. The trailhead is 3,140 feet above sea level.

The Trail

The shade of the evergreen forest can be most welcome on a sweltering summer day; a wade through Cascade Creek near the trailhead after the hike a lifesaver. You'll begin by hiking a bumpy old road along a forested ridge above Cascade Creek for 1.1 miles to the old trailhead and entrance to the Mount Adams Wilderness, where you can pick up a free Wilderness Use Permit.

The road turns to trail at this point, the evergreen forest closes in, and trees grow increasingly larger. Although near Cascade Creek, below on the left, you'll seldom see it through the evergreens. At 1.9 miles, you'll begin a gentle descent above two large beaver ponds and wetlands near the headwaters of Cascade Creek. The forest opens here and you can look west across the wetlands to the beginning of Stagman Ridge. The trail drops, then climbs gently to a footbridge crossing of one branch of Cascade Creek, 2.1 miles from the trailhead.

Beyond, the trail meanders along the valley floor to a second creek crossing, 3.0 miles from the trailhead. Cross the creek and begin climbing more steeply along a wide ridge above the main branch of Cascade Creek. The trail switches back twice, traverses above the creek, then switches back and drops steeply to its end in a swampy forest, 3.8 miles from the trailhead.

Trail's end is likely to be buggy in the summer, with mosquitoes almost large enough to carry your daypack. It's not nearly so pleasant a picnic site as the creek crossings back down the trail.

60. Horseshoe Meadow

RATING	🚶🚶🚶
DISTANCE	9.4 miles round-trip
HIKING TIME	5 hours
ELEVATION GAIN	1,720 feet
HIGH POINT	5,920 feet
DIFFICULTY LEVEL	Difficult
BEST SEASON	Summer, fall
PERMITS/CONTACT	Northwest Forest Pass and free Wilderness Use Permit required/ Mount Adams Ranger District, (509) 395-3400
MAPS	USGS Mount Adams West; Green Trails Mount Adams West 366
TRAIL NOTES	Leashed dogs okay

The Hike

This is a relatively tough climb beginning in a clear-cut area that yields spectacular views of Mount Adams and Avalanche and White Salmon Glaciers, including the remnants of a massive slide on the west face of the volcano.

Getting There

From Trout Lake, drive north at the Y intersection on Forest Road 23 for 1.2 miles to its junction with FR 80, bear left on FR 23 for 7.9 miles to its junction with FR 8031. Turn right and drive 0.4 mile to the junction with FR 8031-070, then turn left and follow FR 8031-070 for 3.1 miles to FR 8031-120. Finally, turn right and follow FR 8031-120 for 0.8 mile to the trailhead, located 4,200 feet above sea level.

The Trail

The first 0.3 mile of this route follows an old road that gave loggers access to the lower flanks of Stagman Ridge. Today, it makes an excellent start for hikers looking for views of the mountain above and Mount Hood, Trout Lake, and the White Salmon River valley to the south.

At the end of the old road, the trail enters the Mount Adams Wilderness, where you can issue yourself a free Wilderness Use Permit.

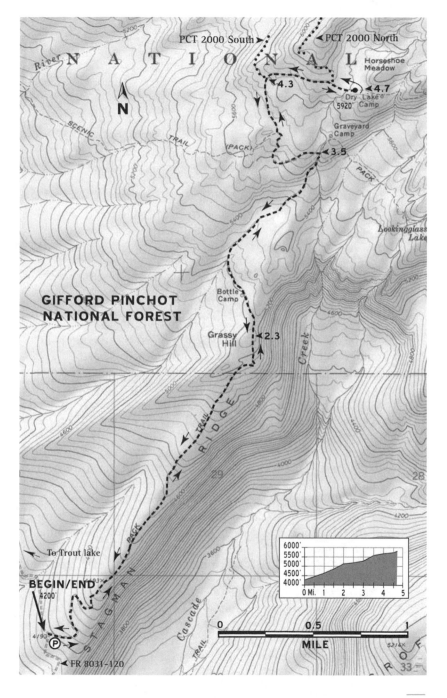

Wildflowers in Horseshoe Meadow include the purple
shooting star and the magenta painted cup.

Beyond, the trail begins a no-nonsense climb into evergreen forest along the crest of Stagman Ridge. In summer, you might hear the rush of Cascade Creek more than a thousand feet below the steep northeast face of the ridge.

You'll continue to climb along the ridge crest and at 2.3 miles, cross the 5,240-foot crest of Grassy Hill—a good turnaround point for families with younger children. The trail descends slightly and passes an old camp, then crosses a stream that in early summer makes a good water stop for those with filter bottles or pumps. The way climbs more gently through forest and meadow, eventually switching back at an abandoned trail junction 3.5 miles from the trailhead.

Here, you'd begin to climb more steeply again to a junction with the Pacific Crest Trail 2000, 4.3 miles from the trailhead. Turn right and follow the PCT for 0.3 mile as it makes a climbing traverse to flower-filled Horseshoe Meadows. The PCT turns north here; continue right another 0.1 mile to the heart of the meadows on the Round-the-Mountain Trail No. 9 where you reach the turnaround point at 4.7 miles.

Sit. Picnic. Ogle the 12,276-foot summit of Mount Adams above.

Going Farther

Strong hikers can follow the Round-the-Mountain Trail No. 9 for 1.0 mile east to a junction with the Looking Glass Lake Trail, turn right and descend for 0.9 mile to tiny Looking Glass Lake, a popular watering hole in the summer. A round-trip hike to the lake would be a strenuous 13.2 miles.

61. Snipes Mountain Trail No. 11

RATING	🚶🚶🚶
DISTANCE	11.4 miles round-trip
HIKING TIME	6 hours
ELEVATION GAIN	2,500 feet
HIGH POINT	6,300 feet
DIFFICULTY LEVEL	Difficult
BEST SEASON	Summer, fall
PERMITS/CONTACT	Northwest Forest Pass required/ Mount Adams Ranger District, (509) 395-3400
MAPS	USGS Mount Adams East; Green Trails Mount Adams West 366
TRAIL NOTES	Leashed dogs okay; mountain bikes permitted on lower 2.7 miles of Trail No. 11

The Hike

Here's a long, dry climb beside a 4-mile-long lava bed that ends in alpine meadows filled with wildflowers and views of most of the civilized galaxy—or nearly so. A car-key exchange and one-way walk is possible with hikers taking the Bird Creek Meadows route (see hike #56).

Getting There

From Trout Lake, drive north at the Y intersection on Forest Road 23 for 1.3 miles to its junction with FR 80, bear right on FR 80 and drive 0.7 mile to FR 82, bear right and follow FR 82 for 2.8 miles to FR 8225, turn left and take FR 8225 for 3 miles to FR 8225-150. Turn left and drive 0.7 mile to the trailhead, located at 3,800 feet above sea level.

The Trail

Water can be scarce on this trail in late summer and fall. Begin your hike by rounding the lower end of the Aiken Lava Bed, a half-mile-wide river of rock that flowed down the slopes of Mount Adams at least two thousand years ago. Despite this hike's name, you'll skirt Snipes Mountain—named after an early cattleman—by about a mile.

Snipes Mountain Trail descends through alpine meadows
and passes the Aiken Lava Bed.

Snipes Mountain Trail No. 11 climbs along the east side of the lava bed in pine forest and across rocky slopes for 2.7 miles to a junction with the Pine Way Trail No. 71. Mountain bike riders must turn right here, but wilderness pedestrians can continue climbing Snipes Mountain Trail No. 11 for another 3.0 miles to splendid alpine meadows at the edge of Bird Creek.

In midsummer Gotchen Creek provides water for hikers who carry filter pumps or bottles, and snowfields often linger through mid-July. The trail is marked in the meadows by large log cairns. The views of Mount Adams from the meadows are inspiring. Look south to Trout Lake and the White Salmon River valley to Mount Hood.

Going Farther

Actually, you won't have to go as far. A one-way hike is possible for hikers with two cars, leaving Snipes Mountain trailhead and the Bird Creek Meadows trailhead. You can arrange to meet at the junctions of Snipes Mountain Trail No. 11 and Round-the-Mountain Trail No. 9 and trade car keys. Total one-way distance is 9.2 miles.

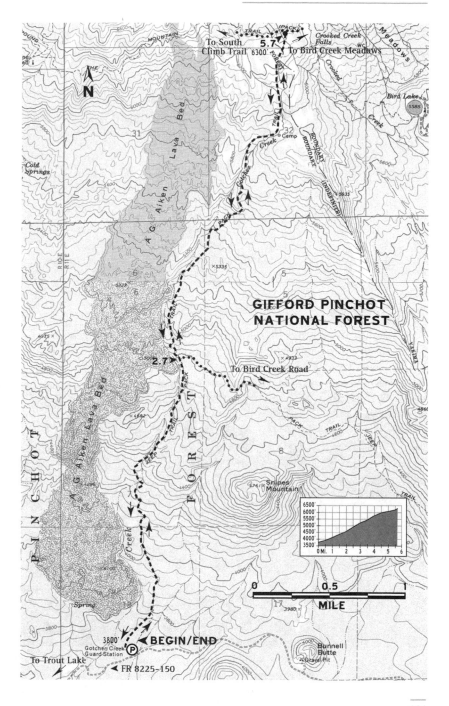

62. Mineral Springs Loop

RATING	 (hiker icons)
DISTANCE	2.1 miles round-trip
HIKING TIME	1 hour
ELEVATION GAIN	200 feet
HIGH POINT	1,430 feet
DIFFICULTY LEVEL	Easy
BEST SEASON	Fall, summer
PERMITS/CONTACT	Northwest Forest Pass and free Wilderness Use Permit required/Wind River Ranger District, (509) 427-5171
MAPS	USGS Wind River, Lookout Mountain; Green Trails Wind River 397
TRAIL NOTES	Leashed dogs okay; kid-friendly

The Hike

Really big trees and mineral springs make this easy walk a good half-day trip to combine with the hike to Soda Peaks Lake Trail No. 133 (see hike #63) or Falls Creek Falls (see hike #67).

Bubbling Mike Springs is one of several found at Government Mineral Springs.

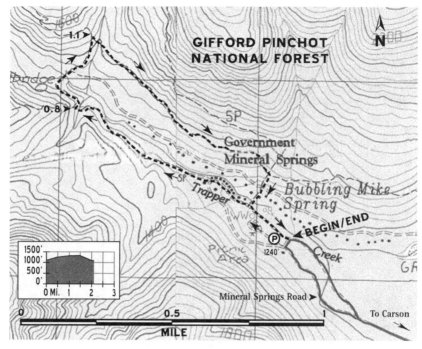

Getting There

Take Cascade Locks, Exit 44, off Interstate 84, about 41 miles east of Portland, and cross the Bridge of the Gods ($1 in 2011) to Washington Highway 14. Turn right and drive 5.8 miles to the Wind River Road to Carson. Bear left and drive through Carson on the Wind River Road for 14.5 miles past the Carson Fish Hatchery and bear left on the Mineral Springs Road. Drive 1 mile to the Mineral Springs Campground and trailhead, located at 1,240 feet above sea level.

Washington residents who don't mind two-lane highway can follow scenic Highway 14 for about 43 miles east from Exit 27 off Interstate 205 in Vancouver. Bear left on the Wind River Road, drive through Carson, and follow the directions outlined above.

The Trail

Huge old-growth cedars and fir shade Trapper Creek on this walk past a once-popular camping area and forest cabins. Park near the picnic shelter and taste the mineral water from a pump near Bubbling Mike Springs, which might better be named Wuss Bubbling Mike for its lack of bubbles. One taste of water from the pump

A sign at the Mineral Springs Loop outlines the history
of Government Mineral Springs.

should do it; it may be difficult to believe that folks once collected water from here to take home to drink, although it might make an excellent slug bait.

Anyway, the trail follows a gated road for the first 0.2 mile, where you can issue yourself a free Wilderness Use Permit. You'll pass several summer cabins along Trapper Creek and climb gently to a junction with the Soda Peaks Lake Trail No. 133, 0.8 mile from the trailhead. Turn right here and drop down to a bridge crossing Trapper Creek.

Beyond, the trail climbs along a Trapper Creek tributary to a junction with the Trapper Creek Trail No. 192, 1.1 miles from the trailhead. Turn right here and cross the tributary, following the Trapper Creek Trail to the east as it descends through old forest to a trail junction above Government Mineral Springs. Turn right and drop to a crossing of Trapper Creek and turn left to follow the gated road back to the trailhead. If you're feeling mean, fill an empty bottle of Evian with water from the pump and give it to your ex.

63. Soda Peaks Lake Trail No. 133

RATING	
DISTANCE	6.6 miles round-trip
HIKING TIME	4 hours
ELEVATION GAIN	2,740 feet
HIGH POINT	3,936 feet
DIFFICULTY LEVEL	Difficult
BEST SEASON	Summer, fall
PERMITS/CONTACT	Northwest Forest Pass and free Wilderness Use Permit required/Wind River Ranger District, (509) 427-5171
MAPS	USGS Wind River, Lookout Mountain; Green Trails Wind River 397, Lookout Mountain 396
TRAIL NOTES	Leashed dogs okay

The Hike

Here's a strenuous climb along a forested ridge that yields peekaboo views of the surrounding territory, leading to a cold lake set in a glacial cirque.

Trapper Creek flows beside the Soda Peaks Lake trailhead.

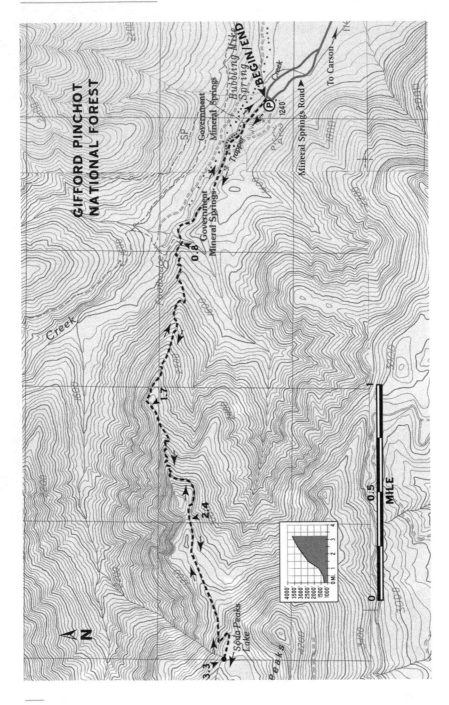

Getting There

Take Cascade Locks, Exit 44, off Interstate 84, about 41 miles east of Portland, and cross the Bridge of the Gods ($1 in 2011) to Washington Highway 14. Turn right and drive 5.8 miles to the Wind River Road to Carson. Bear left and drive through Carson on the Wind River Road for 14.5 miles past the Carson Fish Hatchery and bear left on the Mineral Springs Road. Drive 1.0 mile to the Mineral Springs Campground and trailhead, located at 1,240 feet above sea level.

Washington residents who don't mind a two-lane highway can follow scenic Highway 14 for about 43 miles east from Exit 27 off Interstate 205 in Vancouver. Bear left on the Wind River Road, drive through Carson, and follow the directions outlined above.

The Trail

Unless you are trying to control your fluid intake, don't fill your water bottle from the pump at the picnic shelter at the trailhead. This is the mineral water that made Government Mineral Springs popular with campers and owners of summer cabins along Trapper Creek, all people who curiously lack taste buds.

Follow the gated road from the campground loop east, stopping to issue yourself a free Wilderness Use Permit. Continue past summer cabins and keep left at a trail junction 0.1 mile from the trailhead. The trail meanders through splendid old growth forest and climbs gently to a junction with Soda Peaks Lake Trail No. 133, 0.8 mile from the trailhead.

Turn left here and begin the serious climbing directly up the crest of a forested ridge, gaining more than 1,200 feet in about a mile. You'll get a brief rest about 1.7 miles from the trailhead as the trail crests a false summit on the ridge then begins another series of switchbacks.

Climb steeply for 0.7 mile to a saddle between two evergreen-topped peaks along the ridge, cross another saddle, and begin the final climb, switching back above the tumbling outlet stream, to Soda Peaks Lake, 3.3 miles from the trailhead. This glacial tarn is named "Lost Lake" on the Green Trails map.

64. Little Huckleberry Mountain

RATING	🚶🚶🚶🚶
DISTANCE	5.0 miles round-trip
HIKING TIME	3 hours
ELEVATION GAIN	1,780 feet
HIGH POINT	4,781 feet
DIFFICULTY LEVEL	Difficult
BEST SEASON	Summer, fall
PERMITS/CONTACT	None/Gifford Pinchot National Forest, (509) 395-3400
MAPS	USGS Willard; Green Trails Willard
TRAIL NOTES	Leashed dogs okay

The Hike

Here's an exhausting climb with two rewards: fat, juicy huckleberries in season, and a surprising view of the great snowy volcanoes of Washington and Oregon.

Getting There

From Trout Lake, follow Highway 141 west to the Gifford Pinchot Forest boundary, where it becomes Forest Road 24, for 14 miles to the junction with Forest Road 60. Turn left on FR 60 and follow it to Forest Road 66. Turn left on FR 66 and drive 4 miles, passing South Prairie, to the trailhead on the left, 3,000 feet above sea level.

The Trail

The view from 4,781-foot-high Little Huckleberry Mountain is almost as delicious as the fruit that hangs from the bushes along virtually every foot of this 2.5-mile trail. You can stand on the summit of this former fire lookout and see four of the Northwest's most splendid snow giants: Mount Hood to the south, Adams to the east, Rainier to the north, and St. Helens to the west.

It's a steep, strenuous climb of nearly 1,800 vertical feet, with almost half of that coming in the first mile. It seems as if the trail has an attitude. If there's a saving grace to that first mile, it is the fact that the trail is shaded by deep forest, and even on the hottest of days, you'll be grateful for those big view-blocking trees. The forest and its shade climbs with you to just below the summit.

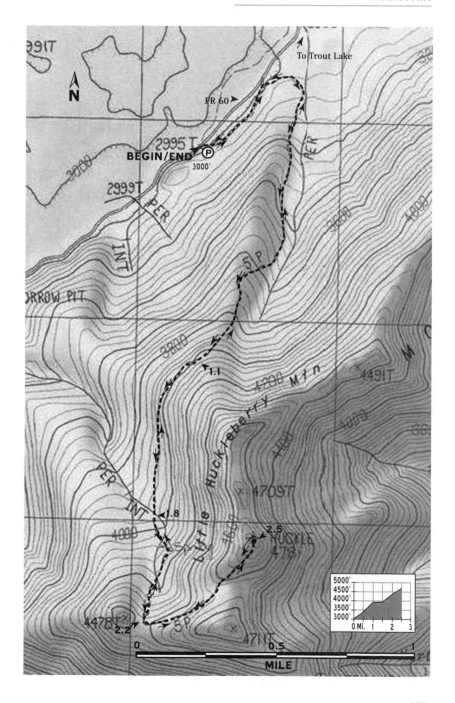

The foundation anchors at the site of a lookout atop Little Huckleberry
Mountain make good seats for viewing Mount Adams.

At 1.1 miles from the trailhead, it's as if the trail crew decided
everyone needed a break and turned to contour along the west side
of the mountain. To demonstrate that forest trail builders are not
without a sense of humor, parts of the second mile of the Little
Huckleberry Mountain trail actually go downhill.

You'll need that recovery time for the final push to the summit,
where the trail again turns uphill at a forested saddle 2.2 miles
from the trailhead. It climbs past a little campsite where you may
find water in early summer, and eventually and quite suddenly,
you emerge from the forest. The fire lookout foundation anchors
make excellent viewing platforms at the wide summit, where
12,276-foot Klickitat Mountain dominates the skyline.

65. Blue Lake

RATING	🚶🚶🚶🚶
DISTANCE	6.4 miles round-trip
HIKING TIME	4 hours
ELEVATION GAIN	700 feet
HIGH POINT	4,800 feet
DIFFICULTY LEVEL	Moderate
BEST SEASON	Summer
PERMITS/CONTACT	Northwest Forest Pass required/ Gifford Pinchot National Forest, (509) 395-3400
MAPS	USGS Lone Butte, Gifford Peak
TRAIL NOTES	Leashed dogs okay; kid-friendly

The Hike

A beautiful high walk that leads through the heart of lake-dotted Indian Heaven Wilderness.

Getting There

From Trout Lake, follow Highway 141 and Forest Road 24 west to the gravel Forest Road 60. Turn left and follow FR 60 more than 10 miles past Goose Lake Campground to Four Corners. Turn right on Forest Road 65 and drive about 9 miles to the Thomas Lake Trailhead. You can also drive north from Carson on the paved Wind River Road to the paved FR 65 and follow it past Four Corners, where the pavement stops about 7 miles from the trailhead.

The Trail

One of the best trails to introduce children to overnight hiking is the Thomas Lake Trail 111, which climbs gently into the Indian Heaven Wilderness for less than a mile before passing no fewer than four lakes and designated campsites. The lakes host big populations of easily caught eastern brook trout and crawling salamanders to keep the kids squealing.

It's splendid high country, 4,100 feet above sea level, where the forest thins and views open. Heading back to the trailhead, you'll see Mount St. Helens through the trees.

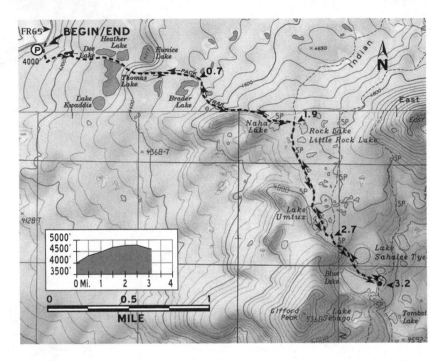

Four of the named lakes in view include Dee, Heather, Eunice, and Kwaddis, just next door to Thomas Lake. The trail continues up a steep, short switchback to a second plateau, passing Brader Lake and a couple of unnamed tarns, then climbs gently to Naha Lake. Just beyond, you'll encounter a junction with a non-maintained path that was part of the Cascade Crest Trail. Stay right and continue to Rock and Little Rock lakes, **1.9** miles from the trailhead, where the trail forks.

Turn right at the fork and continue past meadows and tarns to Lake Umtux, **2.7** miles from the trailhead. A half-mile beyond is Blue Lake and your turnaround point, **3.2** miles from the trailhead. Snow patches cover parts of the trail into midsummer, but most of it melts before the luscious huckleberries ripen.

The lakes of the Indian Heaven Wilderness breed plenty of mosquitoes, so take lots of bug repellent. Most hikers agree—the scenery is worth a few bugs.

Thomas Lake, on the Blue Lake Trail, is a great overnight hiking destination for young beginning backpackers.

Going Farther

The Thomas Lake Trail joins the Pacific Crest Trail 2000 at Blue Lake, where you can turn north or south and wander as far as your legs can carry you. However, it's unlikely you'll be able to day-hike all the way to Canada or Mexico.

66. Race Track via Pacific Crest Trail 2000

RATING	𝕏𝕏𝕏𝕏
DISTANCE	7.0 miles round-trip
HIKING TIME	4 hours
ELEVATION GAIN	840 feet
HIGH POINT	4,250 feet
DIFFICULTY LEVEL	Moderately difficult
BEST SEASON	Fall, summer
PERMITS/CONTACT	Northwest Forest Pass and free Wilderness Use Permit required/Wind River Ranger District, (509) 427-5171
MAPS	USGS Gifford Peak; Green Trails Wind River 397
TRAIL NOTES	Leashed dogs okay; kid-friendly

The Hike

Join crowds of hikers at beautiful Race Track meadow and lake, where Native American tribes gathered to pick berries and race their horses. Shorter, more popular routes leading to your destination mean you'll probably enjoy greater solitude along the trail. Hikers with two cars can arrange a key exchange and one-way walk.

Getting There

Take Cascade Locks, Exit 44, off Interstate 84, about 41 miles east of Portland, and cross the Bridge of the Gods ($1 in 2011) to Washington Highway 14. Turn right and drive 5.8 miles to the Wind River Road to Carson. Bear left and drive 5.9 miles through Carson to Panther Creek Road, Forest Road 65. Turn right and follow FR 65 for 11.3 miles to a junction with FR 60. Turn right on FR 60 and drive 2.2 miles to Crest Horse Camp on the right. The trailhead is across the road, located at 3,450 feet above sea level.

Washington residents who don't mind a two-lane highway can follow scenic Highway 14 for about 43 miles east from Exit 27 off Interstate 205 in Vancouver. Bear left on the Wind River Road, drive through Carson and follow the directions outlined above.

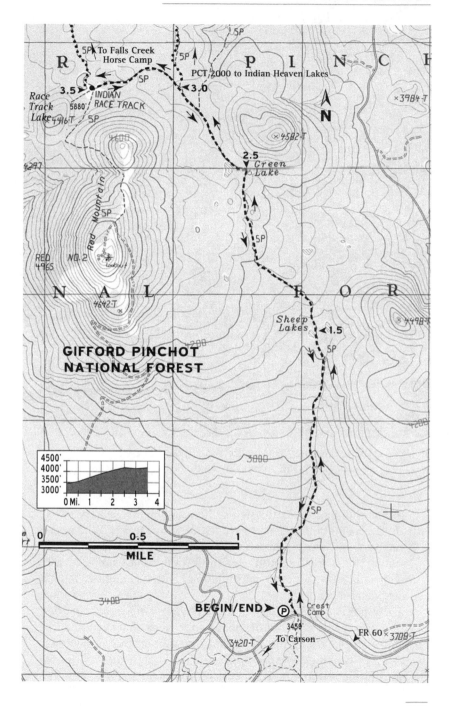

A Pacific Crest Trail 2000 marker along the Race Track Trail in
Indian Heaven Wilderness.

The Trail

A number of paths lead to this excellent late-summer berry patch,
alpine meadow, and lake on the edge of Indian Heaven Wilderness.
The shortest route begins near the summit of the Red Mountain
lookout site, 1.0 mile south—but the 4-mile road leading to that
trailhead is narrow, steep, and sometimes rutted enough to require
four-wheel-drive.

Early fall is the best time for this hike, preferably after the first
frost, which rids the area of most of the bugs that plague all of
Indian Heaven Wilderness throughout the summer. Be forewarned,
however: The huckleberries are so plentiful that it is easy to eat
yourself into a stupor and never reach your destination.

So gird your loins for a long hike, and follow the Pacific Crest Trail 2000 north as it climbs steadily along seasonal creeks that drain Sheep and Green lakes. This path, popular with equestrians, is a gentle climb through pine forest for 1.5 miles to Sheep Lakes, a good turnaround spot for families with younger children. From Sheep Lakes, the trail begins to climb more steeply for another 0.7 mile to the Indian Heaven Wilderness, where you can issue yourself a Wilderness Use Permit. Beyond, the trail levels off at Green Lake, 2.5 miles from the trailhead, and meanders to a junction with the Race Track Trail No. 171A at 3.0 miles.

Leave the PCT here and turn left to walk 0.5 mile into the wide, flat meadow and lake, your turnaround point at 3.5 miles. It's easy to see why this spot was a gathering place for Native Americans for centuries; at some spots in the meadow, you can see the depression of the ancient race track, hammered into the soil by generations of horses.

Going Farther

Hikers with two cars can arrange for a key exchange at Race Track Lake, with one party following the route above and the other following Race Track Trail No. 171 south from Falls Creek Horse Camp, off FR 65, for 2.3 miles to the lake. The one-way hike for each party would be 6.0 miles.

67. Falls Creek Falls

RATING	🧍🧍🧍
DISTANCE	3.8 miles round-trip
HIKING TIME	2 hours
ELEVATION GAIN	800 feet
HIGH POINT	2,200 feet
DIFFICULTY LEVEL	Moderate
BEST SEASON	Summer, fall
PERMITS/CONTACT	Northwest Forest Pass required/Wind River Ranger District, (509) 427-5171
MAPS	USGS Termination Point; Green Trails Wind River 397
TRAIL NOTES	Leashed dogs okay; kid-friendly

The Hike

Walk a forested trail beside tumbling Falls Creek to a splendid 250-foot-high, three-tiered waterfall that rivals just about anything you'll find in the Columbia Gorge.

Getting There

Take Cascade Locks, Exit 44, off Interstate 84, about 41 miles east of Portland, and cross the Bridge of the Gods ($1 in 2011) to Washington Highway 14. Turn right and drive 5.8 miles to the Wind River Road to Carson. Bear left and drive through Carson on the Wind River Road for 14.5 miles past the Carson Fish Hatchery and bear right on Dry Creek Road. Follow it 0.8 mile to Forest Road 3062, turn right, and follow FR 3062 for 2.3 miles to the trailhead, located at 1,400 feet above sea level.

Washington residents who don't mind a two-lane highway can follow scenic Highway 14 for about 43 miles east from Exit 27 off Interstate 205 in Vancouver. Bear left on the Wind River Road, drive through Carson, and follow the directions outlined above.

The Trail

Two trails lead to views of this spectacular waterfall; unfortunately, neither provides an overall picture of the entire watercourse. The reason is that Falls Creek tumbles over cliffs in three tiers and geology conspired to hide the top tiers from the lower tier with a twist in the canyon rock.

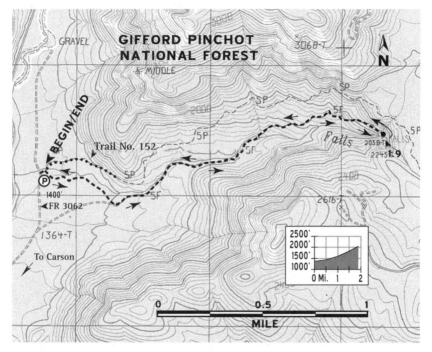

Begin by following Falls Creek Falls Trail No. 152 from the trail-head sign and in a few steps arrive at a footbridge to the left. Stay right and follow the trail upstream along the south bank for **0.5** mile to a junction with Lower Falls Viewpoint Trail No. 152A. Follow this trail upstream for another 0.6 mile before it crosses the Falls Creek at **1.1** miles and begins a steeper climb to a viewpoint of the lower falls, **1.9** miles from the trailhead.

Going Farther

An extremely steep, sometimes slippery and dangerous way trail leads up a gully to the north, near the end of the trail, to viewpoints of the upper falls. Experienced climbers comfortable with exposure can climb all the way to Upper Falls Trail No. 152, about 230 vertical feet above to the north.

A much safer—and recommended—route to the upper viewpoint is to retrace your steps down to the trailhead footbridge and follow Trail No. 152 back to the upper viewpoint. This is a steeper climb than Trail No. 152A and adds 4.6 miles round-trip to your hike, making a total of **8.4** miles.

RESOURCES

Beacon Rock State Park, (509) 427-8265; www.parks.wa.gov

Columbia Gorge Discovery Center, (541) 296-8600; www.gorgediscovery.org

Columbia River Gorge National Scenic Area, (541) 308-1700; www.fs.fed.us/r6/columbia/forest

Friends of the Columbia Gorge, (503) 241-3762; www.gorgefriends.org

Hood River Ranger District, Mount Hood National Forest, (541) 352-6002; www.fs.fed.us/r6/mthood

Klickitat Trail Conservancy, www.klickitat-trail.org

Mount Adams Ranger District, Gifford Pinchot National Forest, (509) 395-3400; www.fs.fed.us/gpnf

The Nature Conservancy of Oregon, (503) 230-1221; www.nature.org/states/oregon

Nature of the Northwest Information Center, (503) 872-2750; www.naturenw.org

Oregon State Parks, (800) 551-6949; www.oregonstateparks.org

Portland Hikers (service of Trailkeepers of Oregon), www.portlandhikers.org

Trails.com (Columbia Gorge and other trails), www.trails.com

Washington State Parks, (360) 902-8844; www.parks.wa.gov

Wind River Ranger Station, Gifford Pinchot National Forest, (509) 427-3200; www.fs.fed.us/gpnf

SUGGESTED READING

To find camping near trailheads in the Columbia Gorge, check out *Camping! Washington* by Ron C. Judd (Sasquatch Books, 2003) and *Camping! Oregon* by Judy Jewell (Sasquatch Books, 1999).

My favorite guide to wildflowers is *Wildflowers of Washington*, which includes plenty of wildflowers of Oregon, by C. P. Lyons (Lone Pine Publishing, 1997).

A book I found extremely helpful in getting me onto the best trails and around the Columbia Gorge is *The Curious Gorge: Fifty Ways to Leave Hood River* by Scott Cook, which is available only at Columbia Gorge retailers (Lynx Communication Group, Inc., 2002).

For more hiking close to Portland and Vancouver, check out *60 Hikes Within 60 Miles: Portland*, 4th Edition, by Paul Gerald (Menasha Ridge Press, 2010).

INDEX

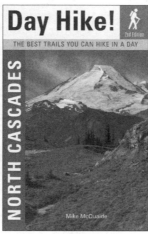